Contents

The Editor writes 3
Sally Smith

Writers in this issue 4

The beloved *Sally Smith* 5
31 AUGUST–13 SEPTEMBER

Clare of Assisi *Helen Julian CSF* 18
14–27 SEPTEMBER

Seasons of change *Ann Persson* 32
28 SEPTEMBER–11 OCTOBER

Jonah *Anne Noble* 47
12–25 OCTOBER

Remembering *Lynne Chitty* 61
26 OCTOBER–8 NOVEMBER

Peter *Sue McCoulough* 75
9–22 NOVEMBER

The season of Advent *Janet Fletcher* 89
23 NOVEMBER–6 DECEMBER

Taste and see *Sally Welch* 103
7–20 DECEMBER

Joseph, unsung Christmas hero *Janet Lunt* 117
21 DECEMBER–3 JANUARY

As a Child: Believed *Phil Steer* 132

Spotlight: Julian Meetings 136
Deidre Morris

Text copyright © BRF 2015
Authors retain copyright in their own work

Published by
The Bible Reading Fellowship
15 The Chambers
Abingdon, OX14 3FE
United Kingdom
Tel: +44 (0)1865 319700
Email: enquiries@brf.org.uk
Website: www.brf.org.uk
BRF is a Registered Charity

ISBN 978 0 85746 308 1
First published 2015
10 9 8 7 6 5 4 3 2 1 0

All rights reserved

Acknowledgements
Unless otherwise stated, scripture quotations taken from The Holy Bible, New International Version Copyright (Anglicised edition) copyright © 1973, 1978, 1984, 2011 by Biblica. Used by permission of Hodder & Stoughton Publishers, an Hachette UK company. All rights reserved. 'NIV' is a registered trade mark of Biblica (formerly International Bible Society). UK trademark number 1448790.

Scripture quotations taken from The Holy Bible, New International Version, copyright © 1973, 1978, 1984, 1995 by International Bible Society, are used by permission of Hodder & Stoughton, a member of the Hachette Livre UK Group. All rights reserved. 'NIV' is a registered trademark of International Bible Society. UK trademark number 1448790

Scripture quotations taken from The New Revised Standard Version of the Bible, Anglicised Edition, copyright © 1989, 1995 by the Division of Christian Education of the National Council of the Churches of Christ in the USA, and are used by permission. All rights reserved.

Scripture quotations from *The Message*. Copyright © by Eugene H. Peterson 1993, 1994, 1995. Used by permission of NavPress Publishing Group.

Scriptures quotations taken from the New International Reader's Version (NIRV Bible) are copyright © 1996, 1998 by Biblica and are used with permission.

Scripture quotations marked (NLT) are taken from the Holy Bible, New Living Translation, copyright © 1996, 2004, 2007, 2013. Used by permission of Tyndale House Publishers, Inc., Carol Stream, Illinois 60188. All rights reserved.

Extract from *As a Child* by Phil Steer, published by lulu.com, 2012

Cover photograph: © Vitaliy88/iStock/Thinkstock

Every effort has been made to trace and contact copyright owners for material used in this resource. We apologise for any inadvertent omissions or errors, and would ask those concerned to contact us so that full acknowledgement can be made in the future.

A catalogue record for this book is available from the British Library

Printed by Gutenberg Press, Tarxien, Malta

The Editor writes...

Welcome to *Quiet Spaces*.

We are leaving behind the summer and moving through that colourful season of autumn and into winter, with its cold and dark, but with all the light and excitement of Christmas as well. It is a period of great change, and we spend some time looking at change in this issue, but not before we have been reminded that we are God's beloved, and that, whatever change is happening, God remains constant in his great love for us. We do more remembering in November through events, festivals and church seasons.

To help us in our journey we travel with three biblical characters, Peter, Jonah and Joseph (Christmas Joseph, not multi-coloured coat Joseph). They are wonderfully real people who show their humanity and behave in ways that are so believable and understandable. It is interesting how similar these three are, although they lived in very different times and were called to very different tasks. I hope that you will learn from them and be able to relate to their humanity. We also journey with Clare of Assisi, who founded a community in the 13th century and is still followed today.

We are then reminded that Advent is a time of preparation and waiting, not a time of spending and worrying and planning. I encourage you to take time preparing for the arrival of Christ and use your senses to get your hearts and minds ready for the birth of Christ.

My prayer is that you find quiet spaces where you can pause on your journeys and rest in God's presence; that you might come to know him more and be strengthened and enriched by the good gifts he has to offer, and that you may become the people he intends you to be. Learn from Peter and Jonah and be realistic before God and with yourself.

Sally Smith

Writers in this issue

Sally Smith enjoys creating spaces that enable encounter with God through leading Quiet Days and creating prayer corners and stations. She has led prayer groups in her local church, works as a spiritual director and as a freelance writer and editor. She has a diploma in Theological Studies.

Helen Julian CSF is an Anglican Franciscan sister, currently serving her community as Minister General. She is also a curate in the Diocese of Southwell and Nottingham, has written three books for BRF, and contributes to BRF's Bible reading notes *New Daylight*.

Ann Persson is a Trustee of BRF. She enjoys using her love of nature and of God's word in the Quiet Days she leads. She is author of *The Circle of Love* (BRF, 2010) and *Time for Reflection* (BRF, 2011).

Anne Noble grew up on Merseyside and studied geology at Oxford and Toronto. She is a Team Vicar in Nottingham and is married with two grown-up daughters. She still enjoys geology, reflecting on what we can hear and see of the God of all time through rocks. In her spare time she loves gardening.

Lynne Chitty was Deacon at Gloucester Cathedral and now lives in a caravan in the grounds of Mill House Retreats in Devon. She combines leading creative writing courses with times of solitude and has a variety of rescue animals.

Sue McCoulough worked for a number of years at the BBC. She was then prayer coordinator at Tearfund. Now a volunteer for the church alliance, Restored, which seeks to combat domestic violence against women, Sue enjoys walking, creative writing and leading Quiet Days.

Janet Fletcher is a priest in the city of Bangor, Church in Wales. She is the author of *Pathway to God* (SPCK, 2006) and a contributor to BRF's Bible reading notes *Guidelines*. She is a spiritual director and enjoys leading sessions and study days on prayer and spirituality, Quiet Days and retreats.

Sally Welch is the Spirituality Adviser for the Diocese of Oxford, working also in a church in the centre of the city. She is a writer and lecturer on spirituality, and is particularly interested in pilgrimage and labyrinths. She has made many pilgrimages both in England and Europe.

Janet Lunt trained in music, composes, creates artwork and leads Quiet Days. She has designed several multisensory prayer trails, which have been used in Bristol, including in the cathedral, and beyond.

The beloved

Sally Smith

Beloved

Introduction

'Beloved' was the word chosen by the Father to describe Jesus his Son on his baptism: 'This is my Son, the Beloved, with whom I am well pleased' (Matthew 3:17, NRSV). It is also God's description of us. It is the core of who we are before God; we are God's beloved.

Yet no matter how many times I hear God telling me I am his beloved, I still often act as though I am not and forget how special I am to him. It is the centre of my being; all else that I am stems from that simple word God uses to describe me, 'beloved'. I am beloved of God. I don't always hear and take this in. It is a message I need to hear afresh daily, again and again and again. I am God's beloved. He wants to keep telling me this.

Reread the last paragraph, making it yours, not mine, reading it as if it were your voice, not mine, forming the words. Note the words and phrases that resonate with you, and those that grate. Receive the acknowledgement of you as God's beloved. Don't be surprised if you keep hearing the same message from God as you work through this section. You are God's beloved and he wants to tell you that he loves you.

The dictionary defines 'beloved' as 'dearly loved'. It is greater than 'loved'. The NIV translates Matthew 3:17 (the end of Jesus' baptism) as 'This is my Son, whom I love; with him I am well

The beloved

pleased.' Jesus was not just loved by the Father, he was beloved by the Father. Beloved goes much further: it goes beyond what God does to me (the verb 'to love') to who I am (I am his beloved—a noun). Beloved is predominantly used as a noun, to name someone or something: I am his beloved.

We don't need to prove to God that he should love us. He loves us despite what we do, not because of it. We cannot make him love us any less; he doesn't stop loving us just because of something we have done. We are his beloved—end of. But neither can we make him love us any more than he does. We don't have to earn his love. It's not a game where extra points are awarded for good deeds. We may please him because of our actions, we may behave in certain ways because of our love for God. But he already loves us as much as is divinely possible.

In exploring the idea of being beloved I have been heavily influenced by the work of Henri Nouwen, especially *Life of the Beloved* (Hodder and Stoughton, 2002).

Love letter from God

Creative

Let us start by hearing the message God has for us: 'You are my beloved.' In the Bible we read this message many times. Because we are all different and it is such an important message, God repeats it, using different language and images to help us understand this love.

Read the following verses, noticing which work for you and which don't. Don't spend too long with each one today. Simply make a collection of phrases that tell you that you are God's beloved. There may be other verses with this message that have been significant for you in the past. Add these to your list.

The beloved

Form a letter from God to you that includes these verses. You might just write them out one after the other, or you may craft them together, creating a love letter from God. You might like to write your letter out and keep it somewhere where you will come across it and be able to reread it often, to be reminded that you are God's beloved.

Joshua 1:9 'God is with you wherever you go'
Psalm 17:8 'Hide me in the shadow of your wings'
Psalm 139 The inescapable God
Psalm 143:7–8 Asking that God not be hidden from us
Song of Songs 2:16 'My beloved is mine and I am his'
Isaiah 43:1–7 God calls us and promises to remain by our side
Isaiah 49:15–16 God cannot forget his children
Matthew 10:29–31 God knows us
John 17:11, 22 Being one with God
Romans 8:31–39 God's love in Christ

I love you

Reflective

You may already have favourite verses that give the message that God loves you, and may want to spend some time with those verses, remembering how much God loves you. It can also be helpful to allow new verses to speak to us and to give a fresh understanding of how we are loved by God, enabling us to have a fuller experience of that love. Go back to the verses in the previous section, 'Love letter from God'. Spend some time with the verses listed in that section, allowing each to speak to you before moving on to the next. Receive from each one the good gifts God has ready to give to you through it. Repeat a verse silently or out loud. Allow it to become part of you, to enter

The beloved

deep into you. Don't try to analyse it, just receive it and the goodness it has to offer you.

You may work through several verses this way, or it may take several prayer sessions to work through one verse, and either is fine. Spend time receiving God's love for you, allowing him to tell you that you are his beloved. Don't rush it—love is not to be rushed.

Baptism of Jesus

Imaginative

Read Matthew 3:13–17.

John the Baptist was beside the river Jordan, surrounded by hundreds of people who had come to be baptised. Imagine the scene. See the people and hear the noise of their chatter. Imagine the river. Can you see John the Baptist? What is the atmosphere like? What are people around you saying?

Do you join the crowd or are you watching from the edge?

Listen as John preaches about the one who is to come, one who will be mightier than John. How do the people react? Do they accept the message or are they fixed on receiving the baptism of John? How do you react?

Jesus joins the crowd, waiting with them to be baptised by John. Does anyone notice him? How do you feel when you recognise him?

Watch John as Jesus approaches and John recognises Jesus. What does he do?

John says, 'I need to be baptised by you, and do you come to me?'

Watch as John (reluctantly?) leads Jesus into the river and lowers him under the water. See Jesus go fully under and as he comes up out of the water the heavens open and a dove descends and hovers above Jesus.

Do you hear the words from his Father, 'This is my Son, the Beloved, with whom I am well pleased'?

You are invited to share this intimate moment of Father, Son and Spirit meeting on earth.

When you are ready, watch as Jesus walks away from John and towards you, calling your name, telling you that you are the beloved and God is pleased with you.

Immediately after his baptism, Jesus is called by the Spirit into the wilderness. Before he goes, spend some time with Jesus, asking him where he is calling you. What does he say to his beloved? And how do you respond?

The light of Christ

Imaginative

John the Baptist's task was to bring Jesus (the bridegroom) and the church-to-be, those who choose to follow him (the bride) together. This traditionally was the role of the best man at a wedding and his task was complete with the uniting of the bride and groom. So John uses the image of the bride and groom and their joining together in John 3:25–30. God our beloved calls us to unite with him, to join with him.

Imagine yourself as a lit candle. What sort of candle are you? Are you tall or small, coloured or plain, patterned, used or new? How would you describe the flame?

Where is your candle shining? Imagine it there. Picture the surroundings. Watch the flame and see the light it is giving. Spend some time accepting your candle and the light it shines, not being judgemental, but knowing it as it truly is.

The beloved

As you watch your light, another light starts to shine. At first it is quite dim, but it soon becomes brighter and brighter. It feels as if your flame is growing smaller. The greater light becomes so bright that it absorbs the light of your candle and the two lights become one. The brighter light doesn't take over, but joins with your light so that they shine together. Enjoy the safety and protection of the greater light. Rest in its strength. Receive from it.

When you are ready, the greater light recedes and your candle again shines alone. How has it been changed by the experience of being in the greater light?

Eternally beloved

Creative/reflective

We are not just called to be God's beloved and to accept the invitation as a one-off event. Becoming God's beloved is a lifetime's work as we repeatedly accept and reject his love and as we discover new depths and facets of that love. God has loved us from before we were born. From before the foundation of the world God chose us in Christ to be holy and blameless before him in love (Ephesians 1:3–4).

God loves us with an everlasting love (Jeremiah 31:3), taking that love through to the future. We are made to be loved by God. St Augustine said, 'My soul is restless until it finds rest in you.'

How do you know you are loved by God today? List the ways. How do you know you were loved by God yesterday? Last week? Last month? Last year?

Think back in time, noting the ways in which you have known yourself loved by God. You may have to do an 'edited' version, noting the key moments in your life when you knew yourself to

The beloved

be loved by God. This should not just be a list of the highlights of your life, however. Often it is when things are going badly that we know God is walking with us, with his beloved in their pain.

It may be that you have not been aware before of God's presence with you in some of the tough times. Can you look back and see now where God was walking with you or comforting you?

You may not previously have acknowledged God's presence in some of the good times, not recognising how he walked with you through those times and the love gifts he was giving you. Thank God for the love gifts he has been giving you throughout your life.

You might find it helpful to draw a timeline of the main events, plotting times you have been particularly aware of God's love, when you have felt strongly that you are his beloved. Notice how God has remained faithful to you throughout your life. If there are large gaps, what was happening during these? Where was God? Ask him for illumination that you may see the story of these times through God's eyes and recognise how he feels about them.

Thank God for his faithfulness and for his dependable love for you. There may be times ahead when it will be helpful to know that God has loved you and will continue to do so.

Turn to the future. Is there a time coming up when it would be particularly important to know yourself as beloved by God and to be aware of his journeying with you, his beloved? Ask God to be there, to continue to love you, and that through this period you may continue to be his beloved.

The beloved

All are chosen

Reflective

When God chooses you, he doesn't fail to choose me.

Do you remember at school that often painful process of choosing sports teams? Two captains were chosen, who were often the best sports players in the class. The captains then took it in turns to pick individuals to make their team. There were a handful of children who were always chosen last. You may have been one of those children. If you were, you learnt at that early age that if someone else was chosen it meant you were not chosen, that they were better than you, that they were wanted on the team. In failing to be chosen, some learnt that they were not wanted on the team but tolerated by the chosen. Or maybe you were always the captain, or the first to be chosen. You were good at the game and would enable the team to win. You learnt good things about yourself, but you also learnt about others that not everyone was worthy to be chosen. How did you feel about those who were chosen last, who might damage your chances of winning? Did you feel guilty about being chosen, aware of their discomfort and rejection?

Fortunately for all of us (whatever your sports prowess or other gifts), God doesn't work like that. He manages to choose each one of us and, in a way we can neither understand nor copy, he chooses each one of us first. So you are not 'a' beloved, or in the top three million of God's beloved. You are 'the' beloved.

God doesn't choose those who are better, fitter, nicer, more holy first. He picks you first. And he does it, not because you are better, nicer, on the preaching rota, do the washing up, feed the poor… but because you are his beloved. He loves you.

Allow yourself time to accept those mighty words, 'You are my beloved.'

Take each word to explore and receive.

You—use your name—not anyone else, you, as you are, the person God sees, the person God loves, all of you. **You...**

Are—definitely, not maybe, no doubt or uncertainty. **You are...**

My—God's, the almighty, creator of the world, omniscient, and he is saying it and telling you himself. **You are my...**

Beloved—loved, cherished, delight, first and last, everything. **You are my beloved...**

Claim your place at the head of God's team.

Mixed messages

Creative/reflective

When you sit in a coffee shop or on the bus and listen to the conversations around you, what is the overall message you hear? It is likely that most conversations will be tales of woe, how badly someone has been treated at work or in a shop, how friends have upset each other and caused rifts and anxiety. It is less likely that they will be praising service they have received, complimenting shared acquaintances or rejoicing at the good fortune of others. When you next meet with friends, notice the balance of your conversation: do you do more moaning or praising? Often the messages we are hearing are that we are no good, that everyone is against us and out to do us wrong.

Similarly, when someone criticises us, we tend to dwell on the criticism far more than we would dwell on praise. We take any slight negative comment and use it to convince ourselves that we are no good, that we are worthless, and the comment only confirms what we've known about ourselves all along. We lose touch with our true selves and start to believe in a made-up version of who we are.

Quickly, without thinking too much, write down who you think you are, your qualities and weaknesses, what you are good at and what you struggle with.

Now bring that list to God, allowing him to accept or reject what you have written about yourself. You might want to start a new list of who the real 'you' is, the 'you' that God sees and loves. Write that list with God. Use it as a reminder of who you are before God and how he sees you, and as a counter to the negative messages you receive during the day.

Ripples from the beloved

Going outside/imaginative

Our belovedness does not end with us. Having received God's love, the most natural thing should be to pass it on. This is not an act of duty, but a consequence of receiving the gift. Having recognised belovedness in ourselves, we begin to recognise it in others and to see them through God's loving eyes. We begin to relate to others and treat them as beloved.

When a stone is thrown into a pond, it creates ripples that spread out to all the edges of the pond. As they travel they grow and alter, but continue spreading outwards. Similarly, one result of our belovedness is that it spreads and touches those around us.

Pause and recall those you have met (or will meet) today; everyone you have had contact with in some form. How did your being beloved by God affect that contact? Which of these people were in need of knowing they are beloved? Which expressed their belovedness to you?

If you can, go to a pond or another stretch of water. Throw a stone in and watch the ripples reach out across the surface. As they reach objects in the pond, ask God that his belovedness may reach those you encounter today. Spend time holding those individuals in God's love and allowing the ripples to reach them as the ripples of God's belovedness reach out from you.

Imagine those ripples reaching to you, God's beloved. Notice how they touch you not once, but repeatedly. Allow God to tell you that you are his beloved, repeatedly.

If you don't have a suitable area of water nearby, take a bowl of water and drop small pebbles or stones into the water.

You may also notice ripples bouncing back from the objects they meet, as God's belovedness is passed on and reaches many others.

My Father's house

Imaginative

Jesus tells his followers that there are many rooms in his Father's house and that when he goes away he will prepare a place for each of them in his Father's mansion (John 14:2). There would be a place for each of them in that house.

That includes us; there is a place for each of us in the Father's house. It is true for everyone. That place is not dependent on what they have done, or how well they have performed. It is dependent on God's love for them and his generosity.

Imagine standing at the door to the Father's house. What does the house look like? What does the door look like? How do you feel as you stand there?

Knock on the door or ring the bell.

After a while someone comes and opens the door. They lead you through the house to a special room. They knock on the door and open it, allowing you to pass and enter the room.

In the room you see the Father. Don't worry if you can't see his features; be in his presence.

What do you want to say to him?

What does he want to say to you?

He may want to show you the place he has prepared for you. Do you want to see it?

Spend time with the Father in his house.

When it is time, leave the house.

You may later want to take others to the house. Take someone you are praying for to their Father's house and leave them with him in the room. Allow him to give them the gifts he wants to give and the gifts they need to receive.

People who call me beloved

Reflective

The voice that calls us beloved comes in many guises. We hear it in our friends and our families. We hear it from our parents and our children. We hear it in strangers and in colleagues, in those we meet once and those we know well. If we are lucky, they have nurtured us and helped us grow. They have fed us and been patient with us in our fumbling.

How often have you wondered what others would think of you if they knew what was really inside you? Would they still take the time and care with you if they knew what you were thinking and feeling? We receive their love but still feel unworthy of that love. We search for some final proof that we are lovable and loved, that we are worthy of love.

Think of those who love you for who you are, not for what you do. Recognise in each one the gift of love that they offer to you. Maybe resolve to show more love back to them during this week, or to spend more time with them. Thank God for their love and commitment to you.

Ask God that you might see his love in them, that they may be bearers of that love.

Broken

Creative

In order to give bread and to eat it, it needs to be broken. In order to share a beautiful cake, it needs to cut. It is in the act of breaking that sharing and giving can take place.

Jesus was broken on the cross so that he could be shared with us. We remember his being broken as we break bread and drink wine together. None of us would want to be broken deliberately in any way, but from the brokenness that happens to us we can draw blessings to give to others. Brokenness is part of who we are and if we offer that brokenness to God, he can use it to help others.

Take some bread. Hold it, smell it, feel it, look at it.

The only way you are going to taste it is by breaking it. So gently, tear off a piece of the bread. Recognise the pain of the breaking, the pulling apart, the rough edges it leaves. Allow the pain of the breaking bread to connect with the pain of being broken you have experienced in the past, or are experiencing now.

As you hold the broken parts, allow God to hold your hands, to hold the broken bread with you, to be with you in the brokenness and to share and carry the pain.

When you are ready, taste the broken bread. Receive the goodness that can only come from being broken. Find the flavour in the torn crust and thank God for being there.

14–27 SEPTEMBER

Clare of Assisi

Helen Julian CSF

Who is Clare of Assisi?

Spotlight

On Palm Sunday 1212 a young woman from a noble family in Assisi went to church as usual. However, this was no normal day but the start of a new life for her. That night, in secret, she left her family home through a heavily fortified door and made her way to a church below Assisi, where St Francis and a few of his early brothers were waiting for her. Clare, now 18, had first become aware of Francis as he preached on the streets of Assisi. She had been captured by his vision of following Christ in simplicity and poverty, and wanted to live that life for herself.

As a woman, this was difficult. It was not possible for Clare to live the mobile life of the brothers, preaching and travelling. Instead, after cutting her hair and clothing her in a simple habit, Francis took her to a Benedictine convent, where she stayed for a short time. Her parents, who had hoped she would make a good marriage, came to bring her home, but she refused, showing her shorn hair, a sign of her consecration to God.

Shortly afterwards her younger sister, Catherine, came to join her. Her parents, even more angry, came with armed men to take both sisters home, but when Clare prayed, Catherine became so heavy that the men could not lift her up to carry her home. Defeated, they left. Shortly afterwards, Francis brought

Clare and Catherine, now called Agnes, to the church of San Damiano, the scene of an important conversion experience for him. There other women came to join them, and the Poor Clare community began. Clare stayed at San Damiano for the rest of her life; from 1215 she was (reluctantly) abbess.

Have you ever made a drastic change in your way of life? Was there someone who inspired you to make this change?

Choosing poverty

Reflective

It was Francis' commitment to poverty which had inspired Clare to follow Christ in his way, and this remained a central value in her life. She didn't simply want to be poor herself, but to live in a community which was poor. The community at San Damiano certainly fulfilled this desire. Food was often scarce. One of the stories told by her sisters was of the day when there was only half a loaf of bread to feed 50 sisters. Clare told Sister Cecilia to cut 50 slices from it; Cecilia replied that the miracle of the loaves and fish would be needed to get 50 slices out of it. But, in obedience, she began to cut, and produced 50 'large and good' slices.

The building too was in a poor state of repair. In 1246, when it was a well-established monastery with many sisters, the main door fell on top of Clare when she was closing it.

However, Clare remained committed to poverty, even in the face of the highest authority in the church. When the Pope came to Assisi for the canonisation of Francis, he visited Clare at San Damiano. He tried to persuade her to receive possessions, because of the dangerous and difficult times in which they lived. He even offered to absolve her of her vow of poverty.

Clare replied, 'Absolve me from my sins, but do not absolve me from following Christ.'

The belief that in living in poverty she was following Christ was the key reason for Clare's embrace of poverty. She was inspired by the words of 2 Corinthians 8:9, about Christ, who 'though he was rich, yet for your sakes he became poor, so that by his poverty you might become rich' (NRSV).

Being poor often means being dependent on others. Use Jesus' words 'Blessed are you who are poor, for yours is the kingdom of God' (Luke 6:20) to consider how being poor might be a blessing for you. Be honest about what you would hate about it too. Can you come to see a value in chosen poverty, as a way of expressing dependence on God? How might you embrace it in one new way this week?

Holy friendship

Reflective

Once when Francis was staying in Assisi, he went to San Damiano to talk to Clare. Although they shared a vision of following Christ and followed a similar path, Francis did not often visit Clare. She asked that he share a meal with her, but for a long time he refused. In the end, however, encouraged by his brothers, who urged him to be generous to the woman who had given up so much to follow Christ in his way, he relented. He decided that the meal should take place at St Mary of the Angels, where she had joined Francis on the night she ran away from home, and had received the habit.

On the appointed day Clare, with another sister, was escorted to St Mary of the Angels by some brothers. When she arrived, she spent some time in prayer at the altar where she had made her vow, and then she was shown around the church and friary. When the meal was ready, she sat down beside Francis, and their companions also sat down together. As the first course was being served, Francis began to speak of God, and he did so with such depth and sweetness that they forgot to eat and were caught up in God's grace and rapt in his love.

Meanwhile the local people came rushing to the place, because they saw flames leaping up. When they arrived, they found no fire but only Francis and Clare and their companions, with their eyes and hands raised to heaven, caught up in contemplating God. The people realised that this was divine fire, showing the depth of love in the souls of these women and men. After a long time, Francis and Clare returned from their contemplation, and Clare returned to San Damiano, greatly comforted by her meeting and nourished by spiritual food.

Have you ever had a friendship which has led you more deeply into the presence of God? Remember and give thanks for it. What qualities in your friend had this effect on you? And how might you become the kind of friend whose company leads others into God's presence? If you can, identify one friendship which could become such a holy friendship, and decide on a first step towards making it so.

The mirror of the cross

Visual

Clare had a particular devotion to the passion of Christ, and she used a very striking image to encourage Agnes to pray with the passion. She spoke of Christ as a mirror, into which Agnes could gaze, and in which she would see the whole life of Christ. Mirrors at that time were made of metal, not glass, and reflected differently in different parts, hence Clare's advice to look into different parts of the 'mirror' of Christ. This passage is from Clare's 4th Letter to Agnes, 19–27:

> For in that mirror shine blessed poverty, holy humility, love beyond words as—by the grace of God—you can contemplate in the whole mirror.
>
> Turn your mind, I say, to the border of this mirror; to the poverty of him who was placed in a manger and wrapped in tiny garments. O wonderful humility! O astounding poverty! The King of Angels, the Lord of heaven and earth, rests in a manger.
>
> Then in the centre of the mirror, consider the humility (not to speak of the blessed poverty, the infinite and costly troubles which he took upon himself to redeem the human race).
>
> At the edges of that same mirror, contemplate the love beyond words through which he chose to suffer on the Tree of the cross and, on that same Tree, to die the most disgraceful death of any.
>
> *CLARE OF ASSISI, VOLUME ONE: THE WRITINGS,* TRANSLATED BY FRANCES TERESA OSC, AVAILABLE FROM WWW.POORCLARESARUNDEL.ORG

Choose a favourite image of Christ on the cross and spend time gazing on it. What do you see of Christ's life held within it? Does it bring to mind particular parts of his teaching? What are you being taught to consider as you gaze on the passion of Christ? Enter into the story and receive from it.

Clare of Assisi

Washing one another's feet

Bible reading

Read John 13:3–5, 12–15.

Both Francis and Clare were passionate about following the example of Jesus. Clare was the abbess of her community, and abbesses often lived quite separately from their sisters; but Clare lived with them, sleeping in the same dormitory, and eating the same food. She followed Jesus' example by washing the feet of her sisters, especially those who were sick, and those who had gone out of the monastery to beg for alms. She also washed the mattresses of the sick.

In communities of any sort—church, family, workplace—there are many opportunities to 'wash one another's feet' by humble service. How easy do you find it to do this? Think of ways in which you are already serving your communities; they don't need to be anything big or dramatic. Imagine doing them for or to Jesus; does this affect how you feel about them? If you are not already serving your communities, what could you begin to do? Imagine doing them for, or to, Jesus and notice how you feel.

All it costs is everything

Meditative

These are the words of a song written by a former member of my community, then Jean Te Puna CSF, based on ideas and images from Clare's letters. Read it slowly and use it as your meditation.

> *Refrain:*
> *Place your mind in the mirror of eternity!*

Place your soul in the splendour of glory!
Place your heart in the icon of the substance divine,
contemplating, be transformed into the image of the
Godhead itself.

Taste and know the hidden sweetness of God,
for all time existing to be found by those who love
the sacred banquet which all may share, if they dare.
All it costs is everything,
a heart open, longing, trusting, giving.

Refrain

Taste and know the hidden sweetness of God,
whose beauty is endless and whose love inflames our love;
Whose contemplation refreshes us, brings us joy—
All our being overflows with you,
O Most Holy, fragrant Lover.

Refrain

(UNPUBLISHED, USED WITH THE AUTHOR'S PERMISSION)

God's created family

Going outside

Although Clare and her sisters lived a life of enclosure at San Damiano, rarely going out, this was not because of a hatred or fear of the world. Like Francis, they would have seen creation as one of God's greatest gifts.

In fact, it was at San Damiano that Francis wrote the Canticle of the Creatures (the source of the hymn 'All creatures of our God and King'). Two years before his death he was already ill and staying in a small hut made of mats in the grounds of the convent. After a powerful experience of consolation in prayer, he decided to write these new praises of God, thanking him for his creatures, all gifts of God in creation which we use daily and who are essential to our life.

Clare and her sisters would undoubtedly have known and used the Canticle, with its naming of sun and moon, wind and weather, water, fire and earth, as brother and sister and mother. The relationship of equality implied in this family metaphor informed community life at San Damiano. Each week a meeting was held at which everyone could speak, and everyone's agreement was needed before new sisters were admitted or debts incurred. This is an example of how our attitude to creation influences the whole of life.

Go out for a walk, or find somewhere to sit outside. Look carefully at the created world around you, from the largest trees and the clouds in the sky, to the smallest plants and insects. They are all members of your family. If you feel able, speak to them as you would to a family member, expressing your love and appreciation. As you go through the day, remind yourself that all created beings are part of your family. How does this affect how you live and the choices you make?

Fighting for the Rule

Reflective

Clare was the first woman to write a Rule for her own community; until this point all Rules had been written by men. However, it was a lifelong struggle to have her Rule accepted by the Church.

Early on, in 1215, only three years after she began life at San

Damiano, Clare obtained from the Pope, Innocent III, something unprecedented—the 'Privilege of Poverty', the right to live without possessions or endowments. Three years later Cardinal Hugolino gave Clare and her sisters a Rule based largely on the Rule of St Benedict, without the commitment to poverty she longed for, but when, as Pope, he came to canonise Francis in 1228, he gave Clare written confirmation of the Privilege of Poverty.

The Church at the time was anxious about new communities and had decreed that new communities had to take an existing Rule—no new Rules would be accepted. The authorities were also concerned that women's communities in particular should be financially secure. It was a difficult time to gain acceptance for a new Rule which had at its centre a commitment to poverty.

Twenty years on, another Pope, Innocent IV, imposed another Rule on the sisters. This rule allowed for common ownership of goods, and an agent from outside the monastery to handle their financial affairs. After three years, however, in 1250, the Rule was withdrawn, as no one seemed to be keeping it!

Meanwhile, Clare had begun to write her own Rule, which was finally approved by Innocent IV on 9 August 1253. Clare kissed the seal on the Rule, and two days later she died. Some words of Francis about his own commitment to poverty, and his desire that Clare and her sisters shared that commitment, are at the heart of the Rule; in the original parchment they are placed at the centre, traditionally the place for the most important part of a document. Clare's lifelong struggle had been successful and her legacy secured.

Spend some time reflecting on what values shape your own life as poverty did Clare's. If it isn't already clear to you, ask God to show you which is the central one. In what ways might you need to fight to keep that value central? The fight might be against forces outside yourself, or your own tendency to slip away from it.

Clare of Assisi

We who were with her

Creative

One of the most wonderful sources for our knowledge of Clare is the document known as The Process of Canonisation. This is the record of the interviews conducted by Bishop Bartholomew of Spoleto in November 1253, just a few months after Clare's death, as the church considered whether to declare her a saint. The main part of the Process is interviews with 15 of Clare's sisters, some of whom had been with her since the beginning.

They told what they knew, through their experience of living with her, of her life, her prayer, her service and her character. The Bishop was very thorough in his questioning, frequently asking 'How do you know this?', and establishing when events happened, and who else witnessed them (sometimes the witness can remember these details, and sometimes she can't, which to me adds authenticity).

The material is rich in stories—of how Clare loved poverty, cured the sick among her sisters and those who came to the monastery, and through her prayers drove away a band of mercenary soldiers who had entered the monastery. Her sisters witnessed to her commitment to prayer and to fasting, and that 'when she returned from prayer her face appeared clearer and more beautiful than the sun'. What shines through above all is their devotion to Clare; it is a wonderful testimony to a life lived in just one place, with a small group of women, which yet had a lasting impact on the world.

Imagine that you have died and that someone comes to talk to your family and friends about you. What stories would they tell, what qualities would they remember? Write your own document, drawing on several 'witnesses' to your life. Offer these stories to God—and also the as yet unwritten stories, for the parts of your life which in reality have not yet happened. What would you like those stories to say? Have a conversation with God about all these stories, written and as yet unwritten.

Spouse and mother and sister

Reflective

In writing to Agnes of Prague, founder of a monastery in that city, Clare used some very passionate language. Some of it may make us feel uncomfortable or puzzled. Try to read these words with an open heart and mind, and allow yourself to be moved.

> Therefore, my dearest sister or—as I should say Lady greatly respected, for You are the spouse, the mother and the sister of my Lord, Jesus Christ—You are so splendidly distinguished by the banner of inviolable virginity and most holy poverty. So be strengthened in the holy service of the poor Crucified One, begun with burning desire.
>
> 1 AGNES 12–13

> Now you are held in the close embrace of the One who has adorned Your breast with precious stones, and offered [You] priceless pearls for your ears, and has completely surrounded You with spring-like and shining jewels, and he has crowned You with a coronet of gold, the particular sign of holiness.
>
> 1 AGNES 10–11

> How obvious it is that through the grace of God the faithful human soul, that most worthy creation, is far

greater than the heavens. The heavens together with all other creatures cannot contain the Creator. Only the faithful soul itself is his mansion and his throne, and this only through love—which the ungodly lack.

3 AGNES 21–22, ALL QUOTES FROM *CLARE OF ASSISI, VOLUME ONE: THE WRITINGS*, TRANSLATED BY FRANCES TERESA OSC, AVAILABLE FROM WWW.POORCLARESARUNDEL.ORG

Is there one of these passages which you would especially like to have been written to you? Reread that passage several times; if you keep a journal you might like to copy it there. Allow the words to sink into you, and receive the gifts which they offer.

Following Clare today

Spotlight

By the time of Clare's death in 1253 there were already 150 monasteries associated with her way of life, throughout Italy, in Spain, Belgium, France, Prague, Moravia and Slovakia, among other places. Women continued to be drawn to this life of prayer and poverty; by the beginning of the 15th century more than 15,000 Poor Clares lived in about 400 monasteries; in 1680 there were about 70,000 in close to 2000 monasteries.

From the 19th century onwards new foundations spread beyond Europe to North and South America, Africa, and many parts of Asia and the Pacific. Although the vast majority of those who follow Clare are Roman Catholic, there are also Anglican sisters in England, and Lutheran sisters in Sweden. Today there are over 20,000 Roman Catholic sisters in more than 70 countries. Clare has also inspired active communities, not bound by enclosure, and even a dispersed Anglican community, who seek 'to bring the contemplative spirituality of St Clare out of the cloister and into our churches'.

In the wider Franciscan family there has been something of a rediscovery of Clare, sparked off especially by celebrations of the 800th anniversary of her birth. Increasingly, she is seen not simply as a follower of Francis, but as a founder in her own right, with her own insights and gifts. In particular she inspires all those who look for a deeper contemplative dimension to their lives—a growing desire in our frenetic and non-stop world. Combined with the challenge to materialism of her deep commitment to poverty, Clare has much to offer those who follow her today, whether by joining an existing community, or taking her as a mentor, example and inspiration.

Clare's gifts in us

Prayer

When you feel ready, use as much of this prayer as you can to ask God to strengthen those of Clare's gifts you already have, and to bring to birth those which you desire.

I give thanks for Clare's willingness to leave all to follow her calling.
Make me courageous in my following of you, knowing that 'all it costs is everything'.

I give thanks for Clare's friendship with Francis.
Make my friendships places where we talk of you, and encourage one another in our journey.
Kindle in us your divine fire.

I give thanks for Clare's passion for Christ.

Make me willing to go deeper into relationship with you, that I too may be spouse, mother, sister and brother.
May I be strengthened in the holy service of the poor Crucified One.

I give thanks for Clare's commitment to prayer, for long hours spent gazing on you.
Help me to find my path of prayer, and to walk it faithfully, day by day.
May I be changed by prayer as Clare was, so that others will recognise that I have been with you.

I give thanks for Clare's unwavering devotion to poverty.
Help me to discern what is central to my vocation, and never to give it up.
May I follow the poor Christ faithfully and with joy.

I give thanks for Clare's service of her sisters and those who came to ask for help.
Make me ready to 'wash the feet' of others, and show me those I am called to serve.

I give thanks for Clare's determination over many years, working to have her Rule recognised.
Grant me the gift of perseverance, to struggle steadfastly for what I know is your will; and the discernment to know when it may be time to give up.

I give thanks for Clare's love of creation, for her vision of all that is made as family.
Open my eyes to see your image in all you have made, especially in people I find difficult, and parts of creation I find hard to value.

28 SEPTEMBER–11 OCTOBER

Seasons of change

Ann Persson

Our book of life

Introduction

As we live our lives we write, as it were, an autobiography, unlikely to be published but known to us. It is not a book of short stories but a book with chapters, each one leading on to the next. There is a thread that runs through. What has gone before gives rise to what is to come. The new chapters of our story use the characters, the relationships and settings from the past and build on them.

During our lives we experience changes; while some are minor and hardly noticed, others are much bigger and cause disruption. Life is never static. Think how boring it would be if it was! Life is movement and, like it or not, we live in the midst of change. There is constant shifting and change in global situations, and the media beam swings to highlight them and then moves on to other breaking stories. There are changes in weather patterns and we can no longer be so sure what to expect. Changes take place in our families, our communities, places of work and places of worship. Even in our own bodies, we are constantly undergoing change as millions of cells die off daily only to be wonderfully replaced by new cells.

Nothing is static. Life is like a mobile caught in a breeze or a kaleidoscope that is shaken to reveal different patterns.

Take a moment to think of some of the changes you have experienced today or yesterday—changes of scene, of people, of moods, of activities and others that will occur to you. How have they affected you?

Autumn, a season of transition

Prayer/reflective

Nature also has its chapters, known as seasons. Summer is behind us and winter lies ahead, and in between is the season of autumn.

A prayer for autumn days

God of the seasons, there is a time for everything; there is a time for dying and rising. We need courage to enter into the transformation process.

God of autumn, the trees are saying goodbye to their green, letting go of what has been. We, too, have our moments of surrender, with all their insecurity and risk. Help us to let go when we need to do so.

God of fallen leaves lying in coloured patterns on the ground, our lives have their own patterns. As we see the patterns of our own growth, may we learn from them.

God of misty days and harvest moon nights, there is always the dimension of mystery and wonder in our lives. We need to recognise your power-filled presence. May we gain strength from you.

God of orchards and fields of ripened grain, many gifts of growth lie in the season of our surrender. We must wait for harvest in faith and hope. Grant us patience when we do not see the blessings.

God of birds flying south for another season, your wisdom enables us to know what needs to be left behind and what needs to be carried into the future. We need your insight and vision.

God of leaves touched with frost and windows wearing white designs, may your love keep our hearts from growing cold in the empty seasons.

God of life, you believe in us, you enrich us, you entrust us with the freedom to choose life.

For all this we are grateful.
JOYCE RUPP, *MAY I HAVE THIS DANCE?*, AVE MARIA PRESS, 1992, USED WITH PERMISSION OF THE PUBLISHER

The year is in transition and change is everywhere. Nature will shortly begin its preparations for winter. and it can have lessons to teach us when dealing with stress and change.

Animals will grow thicker coats and birds will have winter plumage for protection and warmth. Can we develop a thicker 'emotional' coat to guard against over-sensitivity at such times?

Squirrels find food in times of plenty and store it, to feed off in leaner times. How can we build up our inner resources when things are going well?

Hedgehogs, dormice and bats are preparing to hibernate, when their body temperature drops and their heart rate slows down. In a period of stress, how about slowing down for a while and offloading some of the activity that you have become caught up in?

Trees are stripped of their leaves to conserve moisture and withstand winter gales. They are dormant and at rest. In the same way we can learn not to waste energy fighting the difficulties but instead, stand our ground, firm in God and face the storm until it blows itself out.

Birds flock together to find food but also for self-defence, because a greater number of eyes is an advantage in protecting against predators. In challenging times it is helpful to have a support system—friends who will listen and stand with us. Best of all, we can talk to God about it and ask for his help.

Letting go

Going outside

On a windy day in October, I like to walk in beech woods and watch the leaves come fluttering and spiralling down to rest on the woodland floor. I try to imagine what it would be like to be a leaf, bursting from its protective calyx in the spring, unfurling and unfolding, limp at first but then strengthened by the food it receives from the sun and the rain; fluttering in the breezes of summer; held still on languid, hot days; observing the birds and squirrels that nest, hide and take shelter in the trees; having its food supply cut off in the autumn until one day, as a result of a weakened stem and a gust of wind, the leaf lets go and descends from its lofty perch to the ground below. There it will be broken down by bacteria until it rots and adds its nutrients to the humus, which in turn will nourish the tree on which it once grew and had life.

Autumn is a necessary transition between the fruitfulness of summer and the new life of spring. No new growth will come unless autumn agrees to let go of what has been. It is the same in our lives. We cannot grow and develop without change. Life events that tear at our securities are like dying leaves. We would prefer to cling to the known, even though it might be unhappy and far from life-giving. But when we surrender to the process of change, rather than running away from it in fear, growth will happen and new possibilities will open up.

ANN PERSSON, *TIME FOR REFLECTION*, BRF 2011

Go for a walk in a wood or wherever there is a tree. Choose a leaf to take home with you. Let it keep you company in your place of prayer throughout the season of autumn. Let it speak to you about your own need to surrender and let go when appropriate, that the new may come.

From one thing to another

Creative

It is fundamental to the human condition that we live with change.

We have all arrived where we are today because of a series of changes:

- From the womb to the shock of birth.
- From babyhood to becoming independent little beings who feed ourselves, walk and communicate.
- From being at home to going to school and learning new skills.
- At puberty our bodies undergo changes and lead us to sexual maturity.

- Then can follow college, university, apprenticeship or getting a job, which perhaps gives us financial independence.
- A big change occurs if we join our life to another's in marriage or some form of commitment. This calls for adjustments, and presents many challenges as well as joys and blessings.
- From being 'the two of us' to becoming parents is another major change to negotiate.
- The cycle begins again, but we are a generation on, and there are more changes to face because there are more family members who closely affect our lives, including ageing parents and children who eventually leave home, emptying the nest.
- Women's bodies undergo another change at the time of the menopause and they enter a different phase in life.
- There is a change from the workplace to retirement, with new possibilities but also big adjustments.
- Then comes the challenge of the ageing process, which is not easy for us. Having been independent for most of our lives, we may have to face the prospect of being dependent once more.
- Ultimately we face death, which is a passage to new life.

ANN PERSSON, *TIME FOR REFLECTION*, BRF 2011

These are all chapters in our autobiographical book of life. Take a large piece of paper, or two or more that can be taped together, and draw a line horizontally across the middle of the page. Mark the line off into five-year intervals. Now turn it round so that it is vertical and begin to write down, on one side of the line, the changes that have occurred in your life. Return to the start and, using another coloured pen, draw a line over your writing that reflects the ups and downs, the emotional highs and lows of those changes. Keep your completed piece of paper so that you can add to it in a later exercise.

Seasons of change

The journey of faith

Creative

Just as there is a human journey through life, so is there a journey of faith. It may have had a clear beginning, a specific time when we handed our lives over to God and began our Christian walk with him, or we may have experienced a gentle slide towards God and an unfolding of our understanding of him and his ways. For those of us who grow up in an overtly Christian family, this is often how it is. We may begin with a simple, childlike faith that takes and believes everything that has been taught or handed down to us.

Later, as in the adolescent stage of life, we may begin to question what we have been taught and even move into a period of doubt. This is healthy if our desire is to get at the truth but it can also be negative if we allow it to lead us away from God.

At some point we move into the equivalent of the adult stage in our Christian life, and at this stage we have amassed experience which strengthens our faith. We will not lose the elements of childlike faith and questioning, but they will not be dominant. We can live with uncertainties and the mystery of God.

The life of faith is a process of continual change and movement in the ways that we experience it and the ways that we express it. It will inevitably be shaped by life's experiences and the dark times are often the times that also take us to a deeper level in our relationship with God.

Return to the map of your life journey and, using a different colour, trace the line of your faith journey—the highs and the lows; the times of revelation and the times of the seeming absence of God.

Unchanging God

Bible reading/prayer

Every good gift and every perfect gift is from above, coming down from the Father of the heavenly lights, who does not change like shifting shadows.
JAMES 1:17, NIV

The grass withers, the flowers fall, but the word of our God endures for ever.
ISAIAH 40:8

This is the background to which we are invited to live our lives. God, who is unchanging, is both transcendent, far beyond our imagining, but also intimate—as close to us as our breath. I am subject to moods both of elation and of desolation. I can feel cross, loving, disheartened, a failure or a success. My life is filled with people who are also subject to moods, and we often bump up against each other. It is like living in a room filled with furniture and obstacles that we try to negotiate, not always successfully. But our God is subject to none of these moods and what is more, he is always 100 per cent for us.

Take some time to let yourself become quiet and still and then to focus on the unchanging God. 'Jesus Christ is the same yesterday and today and forever' (Hebrews 13:8). Gently connect with the One who is for you, who is in love with you and who is ever the same in a world that changes constantly. Bring that experience back with you into the changes that will face you today.

Seasons of change

Changes that we would not have chosen

Prayer

Some changes are under our control—our choice of a career, for example, of a partner, a home and location, changing jobs and retirement. Some are thrust upon us—a move when we were growing up because of a parent's change of job; perhaps, sadly, parents divorcing; redundancy at work; an accident; being faced with bereavement; being depended on for care; becoming ill ourselves or incapacitated in some way or simply growing old.

I have been impressed talking to some elderly people who, having led active lives, are facing up to imposed limitations, due to lack of energy or failing health. One, a retired bishop, told me that in his latter years he had decided to leave the public arena in order to devote himself to prayer and to preparing for the greatest adventure of all. He was content. Another, aged 82, said that she had decided to retire formally and simply enjoy what she most liked doing, which might be painting or anything else that took her fancy. Another was coming to terms with the fact that she could no longer tend her beloved garden, but would still potter occasionally.

Last year 19-year-old Stephen Sutton made headline news. He had been diagnosed with terminal bowel cancer when he was just 14. At first he challenged the imposed limitation with a bucket list of things he wanted to do before he died, but later he left that to one side and instead set his mind and limited energies to raising money for Teenage Cancer Trust. A friend said, 'The weaker his body grew, the stronger his mind became.' He ended up raising three million pounds, which after his death escalated to over four million. Thousands attended his funeral and gave him the thumbs-up, because he had been such an inspiration. His mantra was, 'When something goes wrong in your life, you don't have to let yourself be defined by it.'

Light a candle, or several, to represent the major changes that have been unwelcome in your life experience but which God has enabled you to come to terms with and even gain from in your inner life and development. It could be that there are changes that you haven't come to terms with yet; you need longer. Be gentle with yourself. However, acknowledging those too and bringing them before God is helpful, because this is part of that journey.

The garden of your life

Imaginative/creative

Take an imaginary walk around the garden of your life.

First, form a general impression of it. How would you describe it: a formal garden, a natural garden, a cottage-type garden, a vegetable garden or an orchard? Draw a picture if this helps you.

Then look closer to see what is growing there. Identify the activities and responsibilities that are, or were, yours.

What is:
… in bud?
… opening?
… in full bloom?
… fruit-bearing?
… smothered by other growth?
… dormant?
… dying or dead?

Is there anything that needs:
... pruning?
... weeding out?
... freeing or feeding?
... changing?
... harvesting?

Imagine the Lord comes into your garden. See his enjoyment at being there. What might he say about it? Will that mean any changes for you?

Listen to him telling you that his desire is to work with you in tending your garden.

The bit in between

Reflective

Often between the ending of one chapter and the beginning of another there is a period of transition—a waiting time, which may be short or protracted. We find ourselves in a place of uncertainty, wanting to know what comes next. It can also raise questions of identity: who am I now, without the context of what has been?

This was my experience on leaving our home, where we had lived for 28 years and which we had used as a retreat house. After taking some time out, we moved into a new house in a new area. We worked hard at 'nesting' and then—wham!—depression set in. I had not grieved for the bereavement of leaving somewhere I loved, a work I had enjoyed and the people I had shared it with. I didn't know who I was without the context of our former home. I was bored. I didn't know what to do. Would there be anything God would use me for now or was I past it?

I remembered wise advice not just to fill the gap with things to do, so I could keep myself busy and not have to face the deeper issues. So I talked to God about it. I told him I was bored and uncertain about the future, but wanted to be available to him. I had an unmistakeable sense of his saying, 'This time is my gift to you. Do what you enjoy. Rest in it and wait.' So I went for walks, read up about trees and life in hedgerows, and waited.

Now I know that if we make ourselves available to God, he will never leave us in a dusty corner, forlorn and useless, whatever our circumstances. For me, a few months later an opportunity opened up to be involved with BRF and life opened out again.

In the uncertainty of transition and in times of change 'show me your ways, Lord, teach me your paths. Guide me in your truth and teach me, for you are God my Saviour, and my hope is in you all day long' (Psalm 25:4–5).

Blocks and resistance to change

Imaginative/going outside

I have just been for a walk. My path led into a copse with a stream running through it which was crossed by a small wooden bridge. The stream was hardly flowing because the winter storms had washed dead wood downstream that had got blocked under and either side of the little bridge. As I stood and looked at the unusually still water, it caused me to think about blockages that we allow to build up which keep us stuck and resistant to change. Some of it has to do with our personality and temperament. I remember talking to two women on the subject of change. One said firmly, 'I don't do change.' The other chipped in with, 'Oh! I like change. I find it exciting.' It is true that when we embrace change, it can be both exhilarating and life-transforming. It can be a gateway to all sorts of new possibilities and areas of growth.

What holds us back from opening ourselves to change? As I looked at the debris that was blocking the flow of water, I identified fear and anxiety as the main causes. We get stuck because we are afraid to move forward. The desire to hold on to the familiar, however stressful and difficult, is entirely understandable, but to move on into the unknown requires risk and trust in God.

In your imagination be beside a blocked stream. What might be the debris in your life that is holding back the water, stopping it from flowing on? Name it and claim it. Is there anything that you would like to do with the debris that is blocking change for you?

You might like to go for a walk to a place where there is a blocked stream. Unblock it and allow change to happen.

In the vale of tears

Bible reading

In Psalm 84:5–6 we read, 'Blessed are those whose strength is in you, whose hearts are set on pilgrimage. As they pass through the valley of Baka, they make it a place of springs; the autumn rains also cover it with pools.'

When our first child, Fiona, died suddenly, aged 17 months, we were directed by a friend to these verses. The valley of Baka is a dry, inhospitable place such as we experienced in our sorrow and distress, albeit with God's comforting presence beside us. There is also an opportunity to use it as a place of springs, not just for ourselves to drink from, but also for others to be encouraged by. Even our tears will be contributory. At first all we wanted was to have our little girl back again and could not think beyond to using our experience to help others, but over the coming months and years, that is what happened. As we allowed God to sweeten and restore us (and we had to do some digging ourselves to find the water), so we found others coming toward us, wanting to share their experience of the death of a child.

As we let God into our unwelcome changes, whatever they be, our landscape will change from being arid ground to becoming a watering hole and we will move on in the pilgrimage of life, strengthened by the love of God and the support of others.

On the eve of Jesus' crucifixion, when the disciples became aware that they were soon to be parted from their beloved Master, for whom they had given up everything, he lovingly said to them, 'Before long, the world will not see me any more, but you will see me. Because I live, you also will live. On that day you will realise that I am in my Father, and you are in me, and I am in you' (John 14:19–20). I suggest that you read those words of Jesus very slowly, and maybe a few times, letting him speak directly to you, not just the disciples.

No change my heart shall fear

Poetry/prayer

I end this series of reflections on seasons of change with a hymn, a quotation and a prayer.

> *In heavenly love abiding, no change my heart shall fear.*
> *And safe is such confiding, for nothing changes here.*
> *The storm may roar without me, my heart may low be laid,*
> *But God is round about me, and can I be dismayed?*

Seasons of change

Wherever He may guide me, no want shall turn me back.
My Shepherd is beside me, and nothing can I lack.
His wisdom ever waking, His sight is never dim.
He knows the way He's taking, and I will walk with Him.

Green pastures are before me, which yet I have not seen.
Bright skies will soon be over me, where darkest clouds have been.
My hope I cannot measure, my path to life is free.
My Saviour has my treasure, and He will walk with me.

ANNA LAETITIA WARING (1820–1910)

For all that has been, thanks. For all that is to come, yes.

DAG HAMMERSKJÖLD, *MARKINGS*, FABER & FABER

O Lord, with whom there is no shadow of turning,
our constancy in times of change,
hold us steady when we feel uncertain;
comfort and embolden us when we feel afraid;
open our eyes to new possibilities and fresh direction;
help us to step out into the unknown,
confident to face the future with you,
who in your love gave your life for us. Amen

12–25 OCTOBER

Jonah

Anne Noble

Who was Jonah?

Introduction

The book of Jonah is found among the twelve minor prophets in the Bible. It begins with the conventional prophetic formula, 'The word of the Lord came to Jonah son of Amittai, saying…' (Jonah 1:1, NRSV). To the audience this identifies Jonah as the prophet of 2 Kings 14:25 who prophesied the extension of the borders of the northern kingdom during the reign of King Jeroboam (c. 786–746BC). From this short verse we learn that he was a prophet and that he came from Gath Heper in the hills of Galilee.

However, we quickly find out that Jonah is unlike any other prophet in the Old Testament. Firstly, the message he is to deliver is for Nineveh in Assyria; this is unique as it requires a prophet to prophesy to a foreign people. In their day the Assyrians were a byword for cruelty and savagery. Jonah is to cry out against the city for its wickedness (1:2). Secondly, the usual response of a prophet to 'the word of the Lord' is to question themselves and God, to ask if they are really the right person, and to admit to their inadequacy to carry out the mission but, reassured by God, to engage in the mission to which they have been called. Jonah, however, runs away to Tarshish. In so doing, Jonah sets in motion the events of the book which, among other things, reveal the extent of the grace of God.

Jonah

As we explore this curious book we will discover the outrageous, pursuing love of God which catches up with those who run away from it and is extended to those who will repent. Perhaps the God we encounter in this chase will surprise us as much as he surprised Jonah.

To begin with, read through the book of Jonah. Note down what surprises you, what astonishes you, what you find difficult and what challenges you.

God of surprising, pursuing love, help me to follow you through the book of Jonah. As I meet you in this strange story, so may I meet you in the places in life to which you call me. Amen

Locating Nineveh

Creative

The city of Nineveh is located in Assyria near the modern city of Mosul in Iraq. It is described as a great or vast metropolis (1:2). Some commentators have it as the administrative capital of Assyria from around 705–681BC until its destruction in 612BC. Though it was not a capital in Jonah's time, it is regarded by some scholars as a representative city for Assyria. In Jonah's day and afterwards, the Assyrian empire was known for its aggression and cruelty. Why would the God of Israel turn his attention to such a place? Why would God direct his attention to such an enemy? We know from reading the book that God does indeed spare Nineveh, and we also know that Assyria goes on to conquer Judah and take its people into exile. Why does God spare these people when they go on to cause such misery?

Where, who or what is Nineveh in our lives? Tarshish seemed attractive to Jonah as a place to get away from God. Sometimes, however, God calls us to serve him in places which are messy, difficult and unappealing; perhaps to people or places we secretly, or more openly, feel to be beyond the love of God. Who or where would you not want to take the message of his love and the possibility of his forgiveness? Are there some places, people and situations you feel should be beyond the reach of God's grace? This may well be difficult, especially if the answer is close to home. It will help to be honest and to know that God will not necessarily call us to go to such places or people—he knows each of our hearts, what we are capable of and what is beyond us. However, admitting that we sometimes feel that there are people and places which might lie outside God's love can be a first step to admitting to ourselves that there are places in our lives which we feel are beyond God too.

What would happen if no one took these people the message of God's love?

Take time today to pray for Christians who minister in difficult places of our world.

If you can, plant some seeds, preferably ones which will germinate and grow quickly, such as mustard or cress. Over the next week, make a note of how your plant is growing. What does it take to help it to grow well? If you have a camera, you could take photographs of it every day. We will return to these plants at the end of our time with Jonah.

Alternatively, place a favourite pot plant somewhere central in your home or make your observations on a plant outside.

Fleeing from the presence of God

Reflective/prayer

Jonah's response to God's call is to run 'away from the Lord' (1:3). The text literally says 'to flee from the presence or the face of the Lord'. In a world where God is present in all creation,

Jonah imagines that he can find a place where God is not present. The phrase implies that he doesn't want to be in God's presence anymore; he wishes to gaze no longer, figuratively speaking, on the Lord's face. For Jonah this flight is significant, and he must have been experiencing some deep turmoil or fear to take such a course of action. Yet, in running, he is denying the chance to the Ninevites to hear about God, however hard that message might be for them and for Jonah.

All of us who are baptised Christians live a called life. What is God calling you to do? What message or action might be your calling in life?

Take some time to reflect on your calling in life and remember that all Christians are called—not just priests! Ask for God's help to stick with the task or way of life he has called you to.

Descending to the depths

Creative/prayer

Where is the deepest place you can imagine? The world's deepest mines are in South Africa where there are shafts and workings extending to over four kilometres. Noting that the word translated 'to board' (1:3) means 'to go down into', reread chapters 1 and 2 and note how often the journey of Jonah is described using words which imply descent.

Sometimes our lives feel like ones of descent. These can be some of the hard moments when, like Jonah, we find ourselves entering the depths of grief, hurt or brokenness. Perhaps this is you today. Sometimes the idea of depth can be a positive one; think of phrases such as 'from the depth of my heart' or 'entering deeply' into prayer.

Jonah uses the depths to try to escape from God, so for him the words are about trying to find a hiding place. He discovers that there is no depth which God cannot reach. This may be comforting to you, or it may seem difficult.

Be assured that God rescues Jonah from the storm and the depths of the sea, going to extraordinary lengths to do so.

In a quiet moment, offer your depths to God: those deep places which are dark, into which you can invite him to shine his light; those depths which represent an intensity that you can celebrate with him; those deep places where you try to hide from God, acknowledging that God is there too.

To symbolise these, you could cut out three squares of paper or cloth: a dark square, a lighter coloured square and a colour of your choice. Lay them out somewhere in your home and hide something small, like a pebble or picture of yourself, under the final square. These represent respectively your place of darkness, your place of great positive depth and your hiding place. As you lay each one down, you might use the following words as a prayer.

At the first square: God who brings light, even darkness is not dark to you. Shine into my places of darkness and despair.

As you pray, place a source of light such as a candle or torch on top to represent God's light shining into darkness.

Remember, 'The light shines in the darkness, and the darkness did not overcome it' (John 1:5).

At the second square: God who understands the depth of my love, help me to accept the depth of yours.

Place a cross on the cloth or paper to represent the depths of God's love for us.

Remember, 'For God so loved the world that he gave his only Son, so that everyone who believes in him may not perish but may have eternal life' (John 3:16).

At the third square: God from whom I cannot hide, enter my hiding places and transform them from places of fear to places where I may dwell with you in peace.

You could choose to move your object from under the cloth to the surface or to leave it hidden.

Remember, 'Be strong and courageous; do not be frightened or dismayed, for the Lord your God is with you wherever you go' (Joshua 1:9).

You could repeat this sequence praying for others or the world as you do so.

The storm at sea

Imaginative

If you can, find a sound recording of a stormy sea. (There are some available online; you could try YouTube.) Try to pick one that lasts for a reasonable length of time. If this is not possible, find a picture of a stormy sea or follow the meditation on its own.

Find a space and become still. Listen to the sound of the sea or look at the image you have found.

Imagine the sailors at the port of Joppa preparing to set sail, loading their cargo on to the boat. The sights, sounds and smells of a busy sea port surround you. You are in a hurry to get away and to hide. You hire the boat, and descend into the hold as far as you can go, hiding behind the cargo. Perhaps sleep will allow you to escape.

Have you ever wanted to hide from God? Do you really believe in your heart of hearts that you can do it? Stay with this thought for as long as you are able.

Now listen as a storm rages outside and the ship around you

tries to tear itself apart. Imagine that you are one of the sailors. This is a storm like no other, for 'the Lord hurled a great wind upon the sea, and such a mighty storm came upon the sea that the ship threatened to break up' (1:4). You race to lighten the load. When life gets stormy, what do you find you can live without? As the sailors cry out to their gods, think about where you turn when life is tough. What really matters? Pray about these things.

Now imagine you are the captain of the boat searching in the hold for things to throw overboard and finding Jonah asleep. What have you tried to hide from God right in the deepest part of your heart? Might now, in the storm, be the place to cry out to God about it? Offer it to God if you can.

Now imagine you are Jonah once again, roused from your trance-like sleep into the maelstrom and disorder. The lots the sailors cast fall on you. You are identified as the cause of the calamity and now you must explain. Owning up to something in our lives, perhaps even confessing our faith, can be a hard thing. Pray to God about those things you find difficult to say to him and to others.

The sailors try their hardest to keep Jonah on the ship. They struggle against a sea which is getting 'more and more tempestuous' (v. 11). Eventually they pray to Jonah's God, the Lord, for forgiveness for what they are about to do and they hurl Jonah into the sea. Imagine the sea suddenly becoming calm again. How do you feel when peace returns after a storm?

The sailors respond with sacrifices and vows to God. This unexpected turn of events has turned them to the Lord. Have you ever had the experience of a stormy part of life causing you to rely more on God? Offer that experience to him now. If life is peaceful, give thanks to God for that peace.

Stay with the feeling of peace for as long as you are able.

Jonah

Unexpected rescue

Reflective

But the Lord provided a large fish to swallow up Jonah; and Jonah was in the belly of the fish three days and three nights.
JONAH 1:17, NRSV

Scholars have spent much time arguing over whether a great fish could really have swallowed a man and kept him alive. Is this strange story literally or metaphorically true? Whether literally true or not, this story contains an amazing truth. God will go to extraordinary lengths to save the one he has chosen to take his message of warning to Nineveh. God has gone to extraordinary lengths to save us too by sending his son Jesus to die, enter the tomb for three days and then to rise again to new life. It is perhaps not surprising that Jesus himself speaks of the rescue mission that is Jonah and compares it to what he has come to do.

Spend some time pondering the amazing grace of God.

Some of the earliest Christian images in the catacombs of Rome are of Jonah, especially of him being spewed up by the fish. You might like to look up some of these in the library or online and think about God's rescue plan for you.

Jonah's psalm

Imaginative/creative

Gather into your prayer space any objects or pictures that will help you to imagine the sea and the 'great fish' from Jonah 2. In contrast to the storm of our earlier meditation you might want to find a sound recording of underwater sounds or a quiet sea.

Settle and centre yourself for prayer, using any technique that works for you. Now slowly read Jonah 2 again.

Imagine yourself into the prayer. What can you see, hear, smell, taste and touch around you? How do you see God? What do you want to say to him?

If you journal or like to write, try writing your own psalm to God. If you are in a good place at this moment, that might be a psalm of praise (similar to Jonah 2:9), or if you are finding life more challenging it might be a cry of lament (see vv. 4–6). Like Jonah's, it might be a mix of the two.

The God of second chances

Creative/prayer

In Matthew's Gospel we hear Jesus describe Peter as 'Simon son of Jonah' (Matthew 16:17). This naming comes at the critical point, following Peter's response to Jesus' key question, 'Who do people say the Son of Man is?' (v. 13). Perhaps Jesus here is drawing some parallels between Simon Peter's journey in discipleship and Jonah's; both have moments of crisis following from decisions either to deny or to run away from God. Both Peter and Jonah, however, are given second chances, Jonah in the recommissioning of 3:1–3 and Peter on the beach on the Sea of Tiberias (John 21:1–19). In both cases there is a recalling and in both cases there is a response, but there are also hints that they still don't quite get it.

The next part of the book of Jonah is all about second chances and the reactions we might have to those; a second chance for Jonah and a second chance for Nineveh.

Read Jonah 3:1–3 and then John 21:15–19.

Spend some time reflecting on these verses: what you have

Jonah

discovered about Jonah and what you know about Peter. What do these verses say about Peter and Jonah? What do they say about God?

Sometimes it is hard to believe that a second chance is possible for us—even a second chance given by God. The scandalous message of Jonah 3 was that it was offered and made available even to a place like Nineveh.

Take an old newspaper, or even today's. Cut from it butterfly outlines; you might want to take these from stories for which you want to pray for a second chance or which celebrate new beginnings. Mount these butterflies on some card (as naturalists used to mount real butterflies). Next to each one write a prayer for a second chance. If you like origami, you could try using your paper that way.

Alternatively, pray for people and situations needing a second chance today. Remember to include yourself.

The scandal of God's mercy

Liturgy

Read Jonah 3.

In chapter 3 we read that Jonah does embark on God's mission, delivering at least part of the message to the city of Nineveh, 'Forty days more, and Nineveh shall be overthrown' (v. 4). The people hear the message and believe God (v. 5). The verb 'overthrown' in verse 4, though, is ambiguous according to some commentators. It could imply destruction, as it was used of Sodom and Gomorrah, but it can also mean to be reformed or transformed. The latter is the result in Nineveh: everyone from the people to the king (and even, by royal edict, the animals) dons sackcloth, fasts and sits in ashes. But, more importantly, they are transformed as people; a feared Assyrian people with a reputation for cruelty turns from their evil ways, and God has mercy on them. There is repentance and then there is forgiveness.

Use the following liturgy to guide your prayers for those places in the world and our lives which need God's love and his transforming power.

A liturgy of scandalous mercy

Lord God...

In places of evil and hatred, we pray for change
May they be transformed by your forgiveness and love.

In places of destruction and decay, we pray for new possibilities
May they be transformed by your resurrection life.

In the hearts of our enemies and those who seek to do us harm, we pray for transformation
May they be transformed by repentance, and your forgiveness.

In the places of my life where I feel prejudice and dislike, I pray for a new heart
May they be transformed by your forgiveness and love.

Lord God, your word can bring transformation to broken lives and systems, your offer of forgiveness can turn hearts from sin to you. Help us to believe it is true, that you really are the God of the impossible. Amen

Jonah

Plant

Reflective/creative

Read Jonah 4. In this chapter we see Jonah's response to God's scandalous mercy. He is not just angry, he is infuriated; his anger burns within him. In verses 2–3 we learn why Jonah ran from God's call in the first place. Jonah was coming up against a conflict between what he felt God's justice demanded and God's mercy, and deep in his heart he had always suspected that this might be the case. Jonah's view of God has been turned on its head. He cannot bear the fact that the Ninevites are not being punished for their evil. Perhaps he feels that God's judgement and justice should outweigh his mercy, even though Nineveh has been transformed.

Pause for a moment. How do you think of God? Have you ever experienced a time when you have encountered God as other than what you expected? What was that like? Was it exciting or perhaps unsettling?

God needs Jonah to see things differently, so he uses a plant to demonstrate to Jonah directly what mercy and judgement look like when they are applied to him. It is an object lesson in grace. When the plant flourishes, it gives Jonah protection from heat and wind; when it withers, Jonah is exposed.

Using the seeds you have been growing, or the photographs you have taken of a plant from elsewhere, reflect on the following:

What evidence of growth have you observed as you have watched?

What have you needed to do to look after the seeds/plant?

Has the plant changed or grown in this time?

Now imagine destroying the plant. How would it make you feel to uproot it?

You might like to use your photographs and thoughts to construct a larger picture showing growth and change. Around them write the words of Jonah 4:2b: 'I knew that you are a gracious God and merciful, slow to anger, and abounding in steadfast love, and ready to relent from punishing.' Read these words slowly and repeatedly.

Gracious God, merciful and slow to anger and abounding in steadfast love, ready to relent from punishing, fill me today with this same love and compassion for those whom I will meet.

Writing the end of the story

Creative

The book of Jonah comes to a seemingly abrupt end. We are not told how Jonah responds to God's object lesson in the plant. From your journey with Jonah, how do you hope or think that the story might end? It reminds me of the ending to the parable of the prodigal son, where we are not told how the elder son responds to his father's pleadings (Luke 15:11–32).

You might try to write an ending to the story, perhaps in the form of a final prayer from Jonah to God (you could use a form similar to that of Jonah 2). If you have time, consider writing two endings, one as if it comes from the Jonah we have come to know and the other as though you were in Jonah's place.

An illuminated psalm

Creative

As we come to the end of our journey with Jonah, we reflect on the journey we have taken. Begin by rereading the book of

Jonah

Jonah. Note down what surprises you, what astonishes you, what you find difficult and what challenges you. You might compare this with the list you made as we began the book.

Now read Psalm 139. For many the words of this psalm are comforting; we feel loved and intimately known by the God who forms us and for whom no place is beyond reach. However, if you were trying to get away from God, this might seem more threatening than reassuring. For others the words are challenging, especially the difficult verses towards the end (vv. 19–22). We cannot run from God any more than we can run from ourselves.

As a final response you might like to make an illuminated version of all or part of this psalm. An illuminated text is one which uses pictures or patterns in the margins as a response to or illustration of the words. If you find drawing difficult, then you could cut images from elsewhere or use words. As you do this, keep in mind the journey of Jonah; this may help you especially when you reach verses 19–22.

O Lord, you know me, all about me. You know what I am thinking and you can find me wherever I am. There is no place that your love cannot reach me, nor any place I might go which is beyond your reach. Such knowledge is both wonderful and fearful for me.

Though I may be afraid or puzzled when you call me, help me to know that wherever you ask me to go, whatever message you ask me to bring or whoever you ask me to be with, you are already there and will be with me every step of the way.

26 October–8 November

Remembering

Lynne Chitty

Time to remember

Introduction

We spend a lot of time trying to remember things—or at least trying not to forget them! In spite of our best efforts, how many nights do we get into bed and immediately remember all the things we have forgotten?

Most of remembering is tied up with doing, but perhaps for the next few days we could remember also to be. Not in a way that is doomed to failure—'remember to find time to be still' is not something we want to add to our daily list. 'Being' isn't a task to be ticked off. It is a gift; a gift waiting to bless and enrich us.

A 'being' time can help us to remember God; to remember those who are suffering and those we love. A time when we forget about rush and emails needing instant replies and mobile phones constantly switched on. A time when we forget everything and sink into the presence of God, even if some days that presence feels more like absence.

We remember that we are precious. That time is not our slave driver. That we don't always have to be in a hurry. That being and doing are like breathing in and out—both of equal importance.

Make time today to sit quietly or to go for a walk, no matter how long your 'to do' list is, no matter how many things you need to remember to do before you go to bed. Be still, and remember that God loves you and that Jesus knew about busyness too. Healing, and teaching about the kingdom was exhausting. Early in the mornings he would find a quiet spot and pray. Amid all the rush he knew he needed to step aside to renew his relationship with and to remember his need of his heavenly Father.

Follow Jesus' example. Make a moment each day to ask Jesus to help you through the day and to say the Lord's Prayer. As you do, may you know God's refreshing Spirit in your life and be renewed day by day.

Simon and Jude

Poetry

28 October is the feast of Simon and Jude, two of the lesser known disciples and friends of Jesus. It offers us an opportunity to remember those we call friends. Aelred of Rievaulx (1110–67), writing about spiritual friendship, said:

> What happiness, what security, what joy to have someone to whom you dare to speak on terms of equality as to another self; one to whom you need have no fear to confess your failings; one to whom you can entrust all the secrets of your heart and before whom you can place all your plans! Friendship heightens the joys of prosperity and mitigates the sorrows of adversity by dividing and sharing them. Hence the best medicine in life is a friend.

Friendship

Friendship is like music,
instruments sharing the same notes,
entwining, harmonising.

Lulls as beautiful as melodies,
played time and again,
yet ever fresh, familiar, faithful, marking special times,
evoking memories, haunting,
the language of the soul shared
amid the silence between the movements.
Harsh notes have their place,
discordant conversations, challenging,
of age and season evoking the notes that once played in Eden,
and will play again in another garden yet to blossom fully.
Music's final gift can never be silenced,
hanging in the air, still playing,
in hearts that miss, but will never forget.
Music unites us in all that can ever be and more.
Friends no longer with us we remember too.
As the music plays and in the long interval when we shuffle and fidget and wait,
we remember.

Peter—a memory transformed

Imaginative

Sometimes memories of failure so haunt us that we lose all perspective and confidence. Peter was haunted by a terrible memory of denying Jesus, of hearing a cock crow. He must have replayed that moment over and over in his mind. He needed to transform that memory from one of failure to one that heralded a new beginning. Imagine Peter on the eve of his own crucifixion as he remembered his last meeting with Jesus.

Remembering

I know I let him down badly. Very badly. But did Jesus really have to ask me three times if I loved him? It hurt, it really did.

It took me back to that awful moment when the cock crowed and he turned to look at me. And I realised what I had done.

There are no excuses for pretending I wasn't a disciple of his. But I was so afraid. It was all out of control. Things were moving so fast. He wasn't fighting them, he was just letting them take him away and I didn't know what to do. It was all right for him, he was the Messiah, the Son of God, he could escape. Perform a miracle. But I couldn't. If they'd got hold of me, I would never have escaped. That would have been it. And so I panicked. I hid. I lied. And like Judas, I betrayed the man who had given meaning to my life. The man who had helped me glimpse the best of humanity, who had made God's kingdom real. The man I thought I would die for until it came to it, and I slunk away like a deserter from a defeated army.

So it hurt when he asked me the third time, 'Do you love me?'

But now, I realise that it was in that third asking that he released me from the guilt and shame and brokenness. When I spoke out loud in passion, in pain, in frustration, and from the depths of my heart, 'Lord, you know everything, you know that I love you,' I realised then that I really did. I really did love him.

I still didn't understand what that might mean. Whether I would go back to my boat and my fishing, or on to a new calling, a new way of living. 'Feed my sheep,' he said, but he was the good shepherd, not me. Was I still the rock? It wasn't until that dramatic day when the Holy Spirit came upon us and I realised the awesomeness of God's power and the depth of his love for his people, and how that would transfigure and transform me, that I understood that there was no going back. The words he had spoken on that first encounter—'I will make you fishers of men'—those words were being fulfilled.

So now I look back, and I look forward and know that in the morning I too will be crucified. That I too will be bound and led where I do not want to go. I know that I really did love him. I am grateful that he asked me the third time, 'Do you love me?', for it was then that I found my voice, my true voice. It will be those words that I utter last when they nail my hands and feet as they nailed his. I am afraid, very afraid, though more of pain than of death. I will not deny him this time. I cannot. I can only speak out with all the strength I can muster, 'Lord, you know everything; you know that I love you.'

What memories haunt you? Imagine Jesus asking you, 'Do you love me?' What might he be calling you to do? Jesus meets us where we are. He met Thomas in his doubt, Saul in his certainty and Peter in his need for forgiveness. Where might he meet you?

Trees

Reflective/creative

As I look at the trees, now mostly bare, I wonder how it would be if they remembered autumns and winters past and knew that new growth would come as it always had. The wonderful autumnal brightness which has slowly faded and now left them bereft is part of a rhythm that will see them freshly clothed in spring with a newness and vibrancy of life. The birds nest in their branches and hope is reflected in our eyes as we witness again the miracle of creation, loss and re-creation.

In the grey times of the year and in the barren times of life, it is hard to trust that there can be a new beginning, that sadness, hardship, loss of purpose, loss of faith are but seasons in life. Though dreadful while we are journeying through them, they will pass, and spring will gradually put out her shoots bravely, like the first snowdrops, and life that has become dark and bereft of joy can know spring again.

Take time to reflect on the winter seasons of your life. Are you in the midst of one now? Draw the shape of a leaf or gather a fallen one from your garden or from a park and use it as your prayer for today. Ask God to bless you with the gifts of trust and hope. Pray for those in your life and around the world who are in need of those gifts.

Gracious God, as your faithful earth weathers the changing seasons and continues to renew itself out of decay, help me to brave the changing seasons of my life. May the long dark nights of winter's starkness not erase the memory of autumn's glory or stifle the anticipation of the gentle bursting through of the new buds of spring. May the trees of creation help me to trust your promise that you are always with me. Amen

November

Reflective

November is the month of remembering: All Saints, All Souls, Guy Fawkes night and Remembrance Sunday. Why is it important to remember together? It's not as if we ever really forget those we love. Remembering is more than just the opposite of forgetting nor is it about rooting us deeply to the past. It is about helping us to live our lives today. It is to make new, to put back together, to 're-member'. That is what Jesus did at the Eucharist.

On the night before he died, Jesus gathered his disciples around a table for a simple meal. He broke bread and shared wine, and said to them, 'Do this in remembrance of me.' The church has gathered ever since, sometimes in hundreds, sometimes in twos and threes, to commemorate that Last Supper. Our faith is both living and an act of remembering, enabling us to look back and to look forward.

Jesus knew he was going to die, but he gave his disciples something to remember individually and as a group of friends. At one level, when we have lost someone, each of us remembers and grieves alone. Yet remembering as a family, as a community, as a congregation can bring us closer together in a profound way. Shared memories can make us cry; they can make us smile; they can give us the courage to go on amid all the confusion and anguish and anger that loss can generate. In our aloneness and in our togetherness, remembering is precious—sometimes painful, yes, but precious.

Whenever we find ourselves remembering this month, on our own or together, as we wear our poppies or as we quietly light a candle, let's remember the past with courage, face the future with hope and encourage one another to live life to the full.

All Saints' Day

Reflective

Light a candle and remember those who, by their lives and example, have been a light in your darkness.

A voice that says, 'Yes, you can.' A hand on your shoulder. A presence that makes you feel strong. A faith that goes on trusting amid pain and disappointment. A heart that refuses to give up until justice is achieved. A love that embraces when others turn away. A forgiveness that allows a new beginning. Ordinary people, extraordinary lives. All these things we give thanks for and celebrate on All Saints' Day.

On All Saints' Day we could think about companionship. Saints aren't perfect; they are men and women like us, called to follow in the footsteps of Christ. Jesus called his first disciples, his first companions, away from their fishing nets to a way of

Remembering

life beyond their imagining. He didn't call them just to listen and just to remember his teachings but to follow and to embody them; to be the kingdom of God in that place and in that time. He calls us to that vocation too. We are to sit at Jesus' feet, but we are also to follow in his footsteps. We are called away from familiarity to new challenges and new adventures, one step at a time. The steps are sometimes big and life-changing ones. We cannot be companions of Jesus and never change.

There have been some wonderful companions in novels. My favourites are Ratty and Mole from *The Wind in the Willows* by Kenneth Grahame. I love their first meeting: Mole has just emerged from his tunnel and stands on the edge of the river bank, a whole new world opening up for him. He hears a voice from the other side calling to him:

> 'Hello Mole,' and he replies, 'Hello Rat.'
> 'Would you like to come over?' inquired the Rat presently...
> Then he held up his paw as the Mole stepped gingerly down. 'Lean on that,' he said, 'Now then, step lively,' and the Mole to his surprise and rapture found himself actually seated in the stern of a real boat!

In that moment of trust Mole took Ratty's paw and they became companions, shared picnics and adventures, accepted the worst and brought out the best in each other. That's what companions do: they inspire each other, they laugh at each other, they cry with each other, they draw each other closer to God. That's what saints do too.

Before you blow out your candle, pray for all those around the world in desperate need of companionship and reflect on the people who you might be a companion to today.

'Do this in remembrance'

Reflective

We have already thought about the word 'companion', which comes from the Latin *com panis*, 'with bread', and reminds us that food and sharing meals feeds more than the physical body; it also nourishes us spiritually and inspires a sense of belonging, generosity and friendship. To eat with someone implies a level of trust with that person. When we invite others to our table, we are inviting them into our home, into our lives. Shared meals can bless and build up relationships. Looking at the Gospels we can see how big a part accepting hospitality, eating with people around a table, being in companionship with sinners and 'high and mighty' alike played in Jesus' ministry. A meal where bread was broken and shared in an upper room was Jesus' last gift to his disciples, his companions, and it was in the breaking of the bread that the disciples at Emmaus finally recognised him.

At each Eucharist, as we break bread in remembrance of Jesus, we share that bread as companions: the companions of Jesus and the companions of one another. It is something to pray for to be known as a companion of Jesus, for our lives to so reflect his humility and servanthood and his grace that others would see us as those who are the companions of the one who invites everyone to his table—whoever and wherever they are. We can't always choose our companions, and saints come in all shapes and sizes. But we can rejoice that we are called by Jesus to be his companions, imperfect as we are, and that he gives us each other for encouragement, through all the irritations, joys and setbacks.

Who might you invite to a meal this week?

Remembering

All Souls' Day

Prayer

All Souls' Day is both a celebration of the gift of life and a joyful remembering of those we have loved. It is a solemn day when we acknowledge the painful reality of separation and name before God those who have enriched our lives, those whose death came suddenly and those with whom our relationships were fragile or difficult.

Let's remember together today as we light a candle for all those who have died young and those who grieve them.

> *When someone dies too young, too soon,*
> *their life seems unfinished*
> *it's as if there is only grief left,*
> *only pain.*
> *Only the question 'Why?'*
> *It's as though all we have trusted has deserted us,*
> *the voice of love has grown silent,*
> *the touch of love grown cold*
> *through the tears,*
> *through the overwhelming loss,*
> *we gently let ourselves think of our love for them,*
> *their love for us,*
> *their love of life.*
> *As we remember all they were,*
> *gradually,*
> *gradually, dawn begins to break through the darkness of night.*
> *Their light, their beautiful light, begins to cast away the shadows*
> *and there is music in the silence*

hope in the desolation.
We remember them not in sorrow only, but in a smile, in a hand held.
We can dare to believe
that death cannot separate us from all they were and are.
They will always be to us our child, our friend, our self.
Though we miss them in the gaping holes where they once were,
yet will their memory bring us closer together.

Remembering Marius the giraffe

Reflective

Marius the giraffe was shot at Copenhagen Zoo in 2014 because he was considered unsuitable for future breeding.

Why remember one giraffe? Yes, he was cute, and yes it was sad and gruesome what happened to him. But an elephant dies every 15 minutes, a family are made homeless every 11 minutes and, most shocking of all, 21 children under the age of five die every single minute. What's so important about one giraffe? What does it matter in the scheme of things?

I think it matters for lots of reasons, the most important of which is because I believe it matters to God. I believe it matters greatly to God how we treat creation. Mahatma Gandhi wrote, 'The greatness of a nation and its moral progress can be judged by the way its animals are treated.' I wonder what the death of Marius says about us? It would seem to me that when animals are treated as expendable simply because they are surplus to requirements or their genes are inferior, it is a very sad day indeed—one to remember and learn from.

Remembering

The gift of life is precious and God-given, and it dishonours our Creator when we take a life casually, brutally or just because we can. We won't all be vegetarians, we won't all have been up at the crack of dawn breaking ice for our chickens or sheep. We won't all think pigs are sweet or rhinos are beautiful. But let us all think carefully how we live, how we treat the animals entrusted to us and how we safeguard their future as well as that of our children.

I remember Marius not because I think he matters more than children, or his death is more tragic than theirs, but because his death asks big questions and most of all because I believe that every life matters to God and every death matters. It is in the nature of love to care, and I believe God is love and extends that love to all he has made.

Bonfire night

Prayer

> *Remember, remember!*
> *The fifth of November,*
> *Gunpowder treason and plot;*
> *I know of no reason*
> *Why gunpowder treason*
> *Should ever be forgot!*

The real and shocking reason why we light bonfires has all but been forgotten and 5 November has become a fun time. I invite you to buy a pack of sparklers and play. Hold in your mind the things that still divide us as church and pray for a celebration of diversity and a healing of past hatreds.

Remembering

A sparkler prayer

As a spark becomes a flame, so may our prayers live.
As the sparks dance, so may we let go of all that holds us back.
As air intensifies the hunger of fire, so may our knowledge of the fleetingness of time breathe new urgency into our love of life.
May the memories of the past and the hope of the future combine to bless our todays.
And may we never forget to play! Amen

Collective memory in the Old Testament was a constant theme for the people of Israel: 'Remember when you were aliens in a foreign land,' 'Remember all the Lord has done for you' was a heartfelt cry from many a prophet. And so we pray:

Gracious God, we remember your church throughout the world.
  We pray for those tempted to use violence to further their cause.
  We pray for peace and reconciliation where there is hatred and division.
  We give thanks for opportunities for communities to come together around shared bonfires and pray for places where neighbours are strangers and many are lonely.
  And we pray we might all remember and give thanks for your love for us. Amen

Remembrance Sunday

Prayers

Eternal God, as poppies sway in the breeze and their seeds are scattered, may your refreshing Spirit breathe through us, freeing seeds of peace and hope, compassion, justice and reconciliation.
  As we remember those who have died in past wars, so we

pray too for those still dying today, and for those who grieve.

We pray for those living in countries where there is civil war, where fear and violence dominate every aspect of daily living.

We pray for those who have been injured and traumatised by the brutality of war, especially those robbed of their childhood by what they have seen or been forced to do.

We remember those who are peacemakers, those who negotiate, and speak out at great cost to themselves and their families.

May God the Father be your strength, Jesus the Son be your inspiration and the Holy Spirit be your guide this Remembrance Sunday and always. Amen

Remember me

Creative

Read Luke 23:39–42.

It is never too late! This reading is a great encouragement that even with our last breath, our last deed, our last prayer we can speak truth, we can acknowledge Jesus as our Lord, we can with confidence face our death, trusting that Jesus will remember us and welcome us into his kingdom.

How would we like others to remember us? What legacies do we leave behind?

Write down five things that you would like to be remembered for and five characteristics that you think you will be remembered as having.

Read the Gospel passage again slowly; speak it out loud if you can.

Jesus, remember me.
Remember us. Amen

9–22 NOVEMBER

Peter

Sue McCoulough

Sinner into saint

Introduction

The Bible contains some great characters. For me, Peter is a favourite—impetuous, well-intentioned and bursting with energy. He features in the Gospels more frequently than other followers of Jesus. Both inspiring and contradictory, Peter's discipleship resonates with those who 'bite off more than they can chew' in their enthusiasm to follow Christ.

The New Testament traces Peter's progress as a follower and then leader before his death as a martyr around AD60. This plain-speaking, poorly educated fisherman became, as his new name (*Petroc*, or 'the rock' in Greek) indicated, the founder of our worldwide church. But his commitment hit some tough challenges before maturing into solid faith and understanding.

Prior to Jesus' death and resurrection, the Gospel writers all depict Peter as someone eager to prove himself who, when tested, lacked perseverance, humility and forgiveness. Jesus himself exposed Peter's naivety and brashness. Jesus' unique example and revolutionary teaching that true leaders must first become servants, putting others first and waiting on God's direction, turned Peter's world upside down.

Peter received encouragement despite his shortcomings, for his role was spelled out to him by Jesus when they first met in John 1:42. However, it's interesting that Peter only worked out his vocation after Jesus had left the earth and the Spirit's power had descended at Pentecost.

Spend some time pondering what you already know about Peter. How easily can you relate to him?

'Follow me'

Creative

Jesus' first call to Peter occurs in all four Gospels (Matthew 4:18–20; Mark 1:16–18; Luke 5:3–11; John 1:35–42). Read all four versions.

Imagine Jesus extending these invitations to you, beckoning you with the words 'Come and see' or 'Follow me'. How does that feel? What response do you want to make?

When recruiting someone, employers write a person specification that describes the person they think would suit the job. Create a person 'spec' that Jesus might have provided when looking for disciples to join him. You might use these headings:

Roles
Previous experience
Daily spiritual practice
Training
Personal qualities

If Peter were applying for the post, what attributes and gifts might he see as suitable for his future discipleship?

Jesus knows that all disciples have different strengths and challenges. For example, Peter didn't have the benefit of hindsight to help him comprehend Jesus' mission. On the other hand, he knew Jesus during his physical lifetime, while we must wait to experience his presence fully in heaven.

Understanding Jesus now is not as crucial as the desire to

follow and grow in love for him: we are promised the rest will follow.

Imagine applying for the post of disciple of Jesus. Write out your application. Notice what you include as well as what you leave out.

Offer the application to Jesus and receive his acceptance of your offer.

Pray with any feelings of excitement or reluctance you have about following Jesus. Peter wanted to impress Jesus with the lengths he could go to in order to prove his faithfulness, but Jesus could only truly 'build' on his life when Peter let go of pride and other worldly concerns, becoming the rock Jesus truly knew him to be.

Stumbling blocks and rocks

Going outside/creative

How was Peter reshaped into 'the rock' for Christ's church? I believe it was through love. When the risen Christ appeared, he forgave Peter's denials. Such love placed an increased yearning in Peter to return his master's love. The building blocks were in place. Following Jesus' example, Peter soon desired to love all people, even those very different from himself.

After Pentecost, his faith was famously made public when the Spirit descended on all believers. The Spirit's impact was to blow open doors to Jesus' kingdom, doors previously jammed by people's attempts to build faith through good works. Peter helped them understand that it's the Holy Spirit who, day by day, truly cements our life and actions into the foundation 'rock' of Jesus.

Go for a walk in your garden, a field or along a beach, and collect some stones. Be aware of colours and shapes that 'speak' to you.

When you get back, clean and dry your stones. You could decorate them with felt tip pens or paints, writing a key word or phrase that you wish to use as you pray, such as 'Be a rock of refuge for me' (Psalm 31:2, NRSV).

As you pray, arrange the stones, singly or in groups. You could use a larger, smooth rock or cloth as a base to assemble your collection. Your stones might represent 'stumbling blocks' to your current walk with God, or stand for rocks on which you're constructing the kingdom. Can you offer up *all* to the loving purposes of the master builder?

Let the Holy Spirit challenge any misconceptions you might have about your contribution to 'building the kingdom'. Remember that Jesus overturned the foundations of expectation on who the Messiah would be, then lovingly showed how humanity would be reconciled to God: 'The stone that was rejected by you, the builders; it has become the cornerstone' (Acts 4:11–12, in which Peter refers to Psalm 118:22).

> *Christ is our cornerstone, on him alone we build;*
> *with his true saints alone, the courts of heaven are filled:*
> *on his great love*
> *our hopes we place*
> *of present grace and joys above.*
> (WORDS: LATIN, EIGHTH CENTURY; TRANS. JOHN CHANDLER, 1837)

Peter's progress

Bible reading/creative

With Christ as the cornerstone of his life, Peter could develop his personal discipleship and 'grow' the church. Hollow promises to follow Jesus (Mark 14:29–31) were replaced by bold words and actions (Acts 4:13) that impressed others and led them to faith.

Peter's 'progress' wasn't straightforward, however. Paul exposed his hypocrisy in his treatment of Gentile believers (Galatians 2:11–14). Peter himself was sent a vision to help combat his former prejudices (Acts 10:26–29, 34–35).

Learning from his own mistakes, Peter built the church by emphasising holiness, or being made clean by God. This meant he wasn't afraid to tackle wrongdoing in the early church, such as lying to the Holy Spirit (Acts 5:3–5, 9–11) or attempts to gain spiritual power through bribes (8:8–24).

At this point, you might like to return to your collection of stones, and think about any representing the church to you. Are any stones missing, such as stones of forgiveness, inclusiveness or openness to discussion? Do some stones need rejecting? These could be stones that embody 'worldly' thinking, dishonesty to God or unloving attitudes towards others. Hold your building before God and listen to him.

End by praying for church unity, while celebrating its diversity.

Peter and transformation

Going outside/creative

We've seen Peter, first as 'a stumbling block', then changed into 'the rock' on which Christ built his church. It's no once-and-for-all transformation. Peter learns that the Spirit's power needs constant reclaiming. He still sins (Galatians 2:11–14) but increasingly prays for insights and renewal. Met by grace, he anticipates final salvation in heaven (1 Peter 1:3–9).

If you have a garden with a bad patch of ground, weed it, then anticipate space for God's new growth.

Or do some cleaning. Pick one section of a room, remove all the contents and put them aside. Look for God in this clear space; has he been squeezed out by your 'stuff'? Ask to refill it only with essential needs or with your most precious keepsakes. God's essentials often prove simpler than ours, so put everything else in a bag for the charity shop. Review the space again. Can you now see God clearly there? What has this transformation shown you?

If you already live tidily, find some area or item that needs scrubbing or polishing.

Conclude by asking Jesus to clear and cleanse all that seems blocked or polluted. The following prayer might be useful.

My Jesus, I stand before you
Willing spirit but weak flesh,
Ego resisting true humility and healing.
Again, I've tried 'going it alone',
attempted to walk on water,
said 'no' to your washing me clean.
Sooner denied you, with a broken heart
than claimed your Spirit's new creation.

You see my puzzled face and ask again, 'Do you love me?'
I wish I could.
Maybe one day.
I will love you.
Help me grow into your love. Amen

Naming and shaming

Meditative

'Sticks and stones may break my bones but words will never hurt me.' This children's rhyme has been used by many parents and carers to encourage youngsters to ignore taunts from school bullies. It might keep things in perspective and encourage us to avoid retaliation, but words have a strong impact on us, leaving a positive or negative sense of identity as we grow older. For example, we feel valued when someone remembers our name.

Jesus calls Peter by different names in the Gospels, some strongly positive, others seemingly negative. Look at the affirming names by reading Matthew 16:13–19. Take the 'naming' phrases from the passage, visualising yourself in Peter's shoes. As you read it, insert your name in the passage.

First imagine Jesus asking you, 'Who do you say I am?'

We know Peter's reply to Jesus was, 'You are the Messiah, the Son of the living God' (v. 16). Do these names resonate or jar with you in any way? Pause before responding to Jesus—instinctively, who would you say he is to you at this moment? Be honest about your feelings.

Allow Jesus space and time to respond to your naming of him. Is his reply confirming, challenging, or both?

Finish by letting him name and bless you, as he did Peter.

The Gate Beautiful

Bible reading/prayer

The ascent of Jesus into heaven could have been a terrible blow for the disciples, but God intervened generously. The Spirit came down to earth, inspiring Peter with insight and authority to declare scripture fulfilled (Acts 2:37–42). With breathless speed, the disciples soon met the needs of many new followers (vv. 43–47).

Read Acts 3:1–10.

We focus now on Peter's next recorded action: the healing of the lame man at the Beautiful Gate.

Recall a time past when you relied on the generosity of others. How did that feel at the time? Did support received strengthen your trust that 'God will provide'?

Now turn to the present. Put yourself in the vulnerable position of the lame man, relating perhaps to any area in your life where you feel worthless, unrecognised or 'unable to move'. Notice how the man makes the first move in seeking help and present your feelings to the Holy Spirit.

Verses 4–6 reveal how the healing took place. Peter urges the lame man to focus on John and himself, as the Spirit works through them. Savour those words of Peter, 'I have no silver or gold, but what I have I give you; in the name of Jesus Christ of Nazareth, stand up and walk.'

In this instance, the power of the Spirit brings one-off, total healing. This miracle is obvious to all: onlookers are filled with wonder and amazement. For us, the Spirit's power might seem to come and go, especially when we take our eyes off where the Spirit is leading.

Today, be bold and invite God's generosity. Aim to do something in a situation or relationship where something has 'got stuck'. It could mean tackling a tricky situation or visiting someone in need.

Begin by asking for wisdom to recognise and remove any blocks to healing action, and that the Spirit alone will be glorified as a result. If you still find 'moving' difficult, shift focus from yourself to the Holy Spirit. Call on him expectantly. Journal and pray with what happens.

Padlocks and keys

Imaginative

Once given 'the keys to the kingdom', Peter could unlock the kingdom of God with authority given by Jesus (Matthew 16:19).

God calls all believers to be key holders and doorkeepers for the kingdom. We can experience opening and padlocking doors, both as individuals and as a wider church.

Begin by placing a candle as a centrepiece on a favourite tablecloth, then arrange any keys you have on the cloth.

When you are ready, light your candle and still yourself before God. After a time of silence, pick up and hold each key in turn, visualising the doors they open and what these represent to you.

Thank God for these 'openers'.

Father God, thank you for potentials given to us
to open doors to the kingdom.
Our keys to that kingdom are so small,
yet you welcome everyone in.
Each key is unique, opening just the right door
to keep out sin and destruction.
We praise you for the privilege
of holding the keys of faith,
and ask that these be granted to others. Amen

Think about the use of padlocks. If you own one for a bicycle or garden shed, you might find it helpful to hold it as you pray. What do padlocks symbolise for you?

Lord Jesus, we pray for those who feel padlocked.
All prisoners, literal or spiritual,
especially those imprisoned by a sense of unworthiness,
or unable to open up to others.
For ourselves and for our church,
we ask to resist padlocking our doors against others.
Help us to lock out ignorance, prejudice or indifference
whenever it seeks to gain entry into our lives.

We ask you daily to turn the key to our hearts,
and come in.

*We ask all these things
through Jesus Christ, our Saviour. Amen*

Now ask Jesus to reveal any locked or padlocked doors in your heart, community or church. Share with friends if you can, remembering others can help us unlock the power of sin, in the same way as doors were unlocked when the church prayed while Peter was imprisoned (Acts 12).

Binding and loosening

Reflective/creative

When Jesus symbolically gave Peter the keys to enter the kingdom, he was giving Peter general authority to use them. Preaching the gospel was one means of opening the kingdom of heaven to all believers.

The book of Acts shows this process at work. With his sermon on the day of Pentecost (Acts 2:14–40), Peter opened the door of the kingdom for the first time. The expressions 'bind' and 'loose' were common Jewish legal phraseology, meaning to declare something as forbidden, or declare it allowed.

Still yourself in God's presence. Breathe in deeply, perhaps mentally saying the word 'binding'. Then breathe out to the word 'loosening'. Allow any images to come into your mind as you repeat this exercise several times.

If you struggle with silence and listening, place a ball of string or wool in your lap. Bind up the ball with each in-breath, then loosen it as you exhale. Take your time. You could pray for certain people to be drawn into the church, as you bind. Your loosening prayers might entreat more people to be Christ's hands, feet or mouthpiece in the world. Pray especially for those boldly spreading the good news of Jesus.

Close your time of silence by reading or praying about those now forbidden to preach the gospel: the persecuted church of which Peter became part. Hold on to the promises of 1 Peter 5:10:

And after you have suffered for a little while, the God of all grace, who has called you to his eternal glory in Christ, will himself restore, support, strengthen, and establish you.

Denial and acceptance

Imaginative

The following narrative imagines Peter speaking at the end of his life while in prison. He's facing crucifixion like Jesus, as predicted earlier (John 13:36–38).

> At last I'm fulfilling my promise—to die for Jesus. Lying here in this stinking Roman prison isn't so bad, for I see beyond these metal bars, to a place pain and misery are old news. The nails they'll drive into me won't have the last say. Soon I'll be with Jesus in eternal glory.
>
> Who'd have thought I'd do so much, see so much—a plain-speaking fisherman from Bethsaida like me? From the moment my brother Andrew introduced me to him, three years with Jesus flashed past like a dream. He seemed ordinary in many ways, yet everything worked together in him to glorify God. You could never predict what Jesus would do or say next. One minute he'd be laughing, telling us stories, some funny, others scary, treating each of us as if we were the only person that existed. Then he'd suddenly rush out to meet the crowds, as if we disciples didn't matter any more.

Peter

I used to feel angry when the crowds arrived out of nowhere. Hour after hour, Jesus let them push and paw him about: total strangers demanding his all. Just when we thought he'd collapse from exhaustion, he'd disappear from sight. Leave us, high and dry, as he went off alone to pray.

Love is a fragile thing, or at least mine was. Once he was captured, I just wanted to run away. Kept excusing myself. I'd done my utmost to protect him, but where was the thanks? More than once he tore me off a strip, and in front of the others.

Those final days I felt shamefaced and angry, then just plain scared. Surely Calvary meant his promises didn't stack up? I should have listened, learned more quickly, grasped the vision Jesus was showing us when we saw him shine, high on the mountain with the prophets. It only started to make sense when he ascended to heaven.

Of course we missed him when he left. But we had our work cut out for us, and his Spirit near to spur us on. Who cared about arguing with the authorities? They couldn't silence us. We were in the midst of many miracles. Thousands were healed, even more brought to faith, both Jews and Gentiles. I'm told some would even walk in my shadow in order to be healed (Acts 5:12–16). By then, I didn't let things go to my head. It only happened because of what my friend Jesus did on the cross.

I've asked the officials to crucify me upside down. I'm not worthy to die the same way as him. I'm still a sinful man, struggling with forgiveness, whether for me or for the other fellow. I asked Jesus, 'Lord, how often should I forgive?' (Matthew 18:21–22). Everyone knows how Jesus answered that. It isn't easy to do.

I suppose acceptance is the key. We're all tainted; all deny or 'kill' Jesus in our different ways. Why should I be 'holier than thou', even about the worst crimes? Being accepted means I'm challenged to accept others, even those who will kill me. I rejoice, and will forgive, overcoming the darkness.

Do Peter's denials/acceptances echo your experiences? Pause to let the Holy Spirit reveal this to you. If it helps, write a list of your 'denials', then aim to counter them with a column headed 'acceptances'. Pray with this list.

Opening out

Going outside

Today we consider Peter's experience of seeing his risen Lord. Against all odds, Jesus was restored to him. Peter surely felt overawed by this new beginning, a glorious dawn after seemingly endless, pitch-dark night.

Jesus doesn't hark back to wrongdoings in the past. He merely repeats one sentence to Peter, three times. 'Do you love me?' (John 21:15–17). These words can invite us too to hear Jesus' entreaty to love, even in dark times and places.

The next exercise is best done early in the morning, before it is properly light. The shortening days should help you! You're invited first to look out of a window at the muted tints of dawn. Now, before God, hold any personal need for repentance or sense of 'absence' you might be feeling.

When you're ready, venture outside, noting colour and detail strengthening around you with the increasing daylight. If you can't go outside, continue peering through the window, noticing particularly any scenes where there is change or movement. Focus on seeing Christ alive, shining out of unexpected places, or in people who pass by.

As you walk, sense Jesus being 'restored' to you. In what ways might he be entrusting things to you again, even if you've let him down? To 'feed lambs' seeking safety or entrance into Jesus' kingdom? 'Feeding' takes many forms: encouraging children at play, greeting the postman at your door, taking a neighbour out to lunch, praying with someone… the list is endless.

Even at this 'dark' time of year, take creation's energy and rejoice with it in your prayer time. Perhaps 'open up' to a friend, or help someone today.

Celebration!

Creative/prayer

Early in his ministry, Peter was miraculously freed from prison through the church's intercession (Acts 12:5–17). We may never experience anything so dramatic, but Christians are promised that God's Spirit longs to be released through them, bringing 'miracles' to our needy world.

Today, you're encouraged to create a 'collage of celebration' by gathering up images and insights from the past fortnight.

First collect images: from magazines, newspapers, the internet or photos you've taken. Stick your cuttings on a piece of card, allowing space to write, paint or draw around them.

Now add any insights, Bible verses or encouraging words you've heard, or spoken to others. Maybe draw in arrows showing the direction of God's healing movement in your life or in the lives of people you know. Make it your celebration of God's spirit moving through our world, opening doors of hope.

With this creative focus before you, invite the Spirit to lead you in celebratory and 'strengthening' prayers. Firstly, for yourself, secondly for specific friends who may be praying for or with you and finally, for the worldwide church.

In the days to come, keep returning to your collage and your praises. If difficulties seem to outweigh the 'miracles', hold on to Peter's experience within the church: lifted up, then able to praise God in all circumstances.

23 November–6 December

The season of Advent

Janet Fletcher

A waiting time

Introduction

Advent is, like Lent, a penitential season, although it is easy to forget that. In many churches the colours, as in Lent, are purple, and often flower arrangements are removed and the Gloria remains unsung. In Lent we are used to the pattern of 'giving up', looking at our own needs for forgiveness, and deepening our faith through a Lent course or other discipline. The weeks of Advent can become swallowed up with the busyness of the preparations for Christmas Day. The penitential 'mood' is overtaken by a build-up of stress at the amount of work to be done, or the joys and pleasure of carol services and wrapping presents.

The story of the nativity is well known, and yet no matter how many times we have heard it before, there is always something new that is waiting to be discovered. Advent is a waiting time. We await the birth of the Christ-child. We await the wonder of God's coming to earth, enfleshed in the skin and body of humanity.

We are all called into this waiting time as we pray and wonder once more about this birth that changed the lives of so many, and changed our lives too. No matter how busy we find ourselves, it is important to make a space in the day to be quiet and to be with God; to wait with God and to wait upon God. We are called to walk through the maze of stories that will guide us, like the new star in the sky, to the stable and to the Christ-child lying in a manger.

Into the darkness a light will emerge.
A light to illuminate the hidden places
where humanity brings violence, abuse and fear to birth.
A light that will reach out, embracing unexpected places
and un-expecting peoples with hope.
Touching into those lives others will not go near.
A light that seeks transformation and renewal
in all who are willing to come,
and seek willingly to come,
to step out of the darkness.
A light waiting to be set free from the darkness of the womb.
A light that will grow as a baby grows into adulthood.
A light that will reveal the sinfulness of humankind,
with the promise of forgiveness and new beginnings.
In these weeks of Advent, I seek your light, O God,
in my heart, in my mind, in my soul,
and with all of my being. Amen

The loving God of Advent

Prayer

In a time of quietness, ponder over your image of who God is to you; the images and phrases that you associate with God. At this Advent time of waiting we come now to meet with the creative God who, in human form, seeks to burst out from the darkness of the womb and into the light of the world, God, who in the Son brings to all the gift of love, healing and the seeds of faith.

Creating and creative God, touch into the creative spring bubbling within me, draw from it the living waters of life, and guide me to discover the potential of all that I am now, and all that I am yet to bring to birth in my life.

Passionate and passion-filled God, embrace me with your tender arms as a mother does her child, cradle me in the palm of your hand, and guide me into the wonder of your desire, and the love you seek to bring to birth in my life.

Holy and healing God, nurture within me the seeds of your healing caress, open the door to forgiveness, refreshment and renewal, and guide me to a maturity of faith and the holiness you yearn to bring to birth in my life.

Loving God of Advent, help me as I seek to be a creative, passion-filled and healing presence in the world, bringing to birth peace, freedom and love. Amen

Ruth

Reflective

Read Ruth 1:16–18, or the whole book if you have time.

If they looked back over their lives, Ruth and Naomi would no doubt be surprised by the way God was present with them, guiding them through their very different lives. Ruth had no idea that the son she would bring to birth would one day, in generations to come, be named in the genealogy which Matthew draws to a close with the birth of Jesus.

Ruth is an ordinary woman, a foreigner, who with her mother-in-law needs to find her place within the community she comes to, and the people she will live among. She leaves everything behind her to travel to a new life in Bethlehem.

Ruth teaches us about loyalty, trust and love for her family—a love that meant she came to follow the God of Israel. With love in her heart she is called by the God she does not fully know, to leave one land for another. In doing so, she fulfils the dream of

God planted deep within.

Our Advent journey has begun, and we are invited to travel with love in our hearts, with loyalty and in trust. It may be that, like Ruth, we are called to leave one place and move somewhere new, not literally, but prayerfully.

In Advent we are called to watch and wait, to leave behind for a time the rush and the busyness of these coming weeks, and instead to come and listen quietly for God's voice speaking into our hearts. What might prevent you from spending time in prayer during these weeks?

Bring to mind a time when you have moved from one place to another: to a new house, to a new job, from working to retirement, from living alone to living with another person. Recall what that time felt like, and then imagine the feelings and emotions of Ruth as she leaves to go to a new country.

A hymn for Advent

Prayer/poetry

It is said that when we sing, we pray twice. This hymn can be read as a prayer or sung to the tune for 'Come thou long expected Jesus', or the verses can be put together in pairs to fit the tune 'Love divine, all loves excelling' (Blaenwern).

Advent waiting

> *Advent waiting, watching, seeking*
> *for God's justice upon the earth,*
> *gathering each and every person*
> *to a love that welcomes all.*
>
> *Seeking healing and forgiveness*
> *through God's love upon the earth,*

bringing freedom, liberation,
ears to hear God's call to all.

Advent waiting, watching, listening,
for God's voice upon the earth,
with a call we are to answer,
echoing worldwide to us all.

Listening, being and preparing,
for God's coming upon the earth,
and in love, God's passion fierce
help us see the love in all.

Advent waiting, watching, hoping
for God's touch upon the earth,
Spirit guiding through the darkness
to the light that beckons all.

Hoping, loving and desiring
through God's light upon the earth,
promise of the eternal Presence
brought to birth within us all.

New beginnings

Creative

Ruth had her mother-in-law with her as she made her new beginning in life, and no doubt new friends too would be made.

On a large sheet of paper, use pencils, crayons or paint to write the names of people in your family you will see over the next month. In a different colour add in the names of those you will not see, and in a third colour, the names of those who have died but remain in your heart. You may also wish to include the names of those whom you no longer see due to a fall-out or difference of opinion. Be as creative as you can be.

Quietly look at the names you have written, and bring them to God in prayer; and in love and peacefulness.

While writing your Christmas cards, you can bring the recipients quietly to God in prayer, asking that God's peace and joy be with them.

God of all new beginnings.
God of my past, my present and my future journeys.
Be with me now in the quietness,
be the stilling presence in my heart,
be the inner courage I need to follow you,
be the touch of surprise which opens from within
the light and love to guide me to Bethlehem,
to the Christ-child and to new life born in me. Amen

The annunciation

Reflective

In the Gospel of Luke we find his telling of the encounter of Mary with the angel Gabriel.

It was an ordinary day, beginning as other days had done, and yet this day had a very surprising outcome for Mary. The Gospel account of the conversation between Mary and the angel Gabriel reveals a woman who does not say 'yes' immediately, but first seeks from Gabriel as much information as she can.

Like Ruth, Mary had a decision to make, one that would affect the rest of her life. She could have said 'no', but at the end of the passage on the annunciation we read the words, 'Here am I... let it be with me according to your word' (Luke 1:38, NRSV). In her saying 'yes', she enabled the greatest wonder and surprise to take place: God being brought to birth in human flesh.

Read vv. 26–38 slowly, and dwell on how you imagine Mary felt during and after her encounter with the angel Gabriel.

Reflect upon a time when you have had an important decision to make, in life generally or in your journey of faith. How long did it take you to make your decision?

What decisions are you making at the moment? How are you approaching those decisions?

Hannah's prayer

Reflective

The story of Hannah can be found in 1 Samuel 1.

Hannah was desperate to have a child. Her husband loved her deeply, but she could not provide the one thing she longed to give him. On the annual visit to Shiloh, she comes to God in prayer, trusting that she will be heard. Her pain and her anguish is revealed through the tears that fall as she prays. Tears and weeping which are misunderstood by Eli. With courage and faith, she puts him right, and Eli then prays for her.

We can all come to God in prayer, bringing to him anything and everything that lies heavy in our hearts. In times of personal prayer, as we seek to journey deeper into God's presence, and as our own vulnerability is uncovered, then it may be that we, like Hannah, find we cry as we pray. Tears can bring a sense of cleansing, of renewal and of hope as we truly open up our inner being to God.

After the birth of her son Samuel, whom she dedicates to God, Hannah is able to pray with joy and thanksgiving in her heart. Laughter and joy, tears and sorrow, are a part of who we are in our humanity, and so they also have their place within our prayer, and within our relationship with God.

The season of Advent

In a time of quietness and prayer:
… think about the prophets of the Old Testament and their trust and faith in God. Imagine yourself as one of the prophets, and how you would feel delivering the words of God, as they did, to the people.
… take time to reflect upon the times when your prayer has been full of joy, or filled with tears or desperation. As you remember that time, what emotions come to you?

Looking ahead to the coming weeks, what may bring you a sense of joy and laughter, and what may bring you feelings of sorrow and tears?

At the end of the time of prayer, ask God to bless you with his peace and love.

My soul awakes

Prayer

Read Luke 1:46–55, Mary's prayer known as the Magnificat.

The Magnificat, known to many through its use at Evening Prayer, is a prayer for all in need in God's world. It reminds us of the heritage we have, going back to the time of Abraham. It is a prayer that is countercultural as it lifts up the voiceless and the outcast of society and brings down the proud and the rich. It draws our attention to the plight of others, and asks us to look at the many ways in which we can pray and support the works of justice, peace and freedom in the world today.

My soul awakes

Deep within, my soul awakes in joy and praise, my God,
for in your love, you have indeed blessed my life.

*My eyes have been opened, and through your holy love
have inflamed my heart to see the world with compassion.*

*You see, O God, the shunned and hated, the hungry and poor,
and you will not rest until all are welcomed, accepted and fed.
Lift up from the depths, from the gutters,
the innocent suffering of women and men in every nation
and do not rest easy until all are free.*

*Your presence is strength to the weak,
and goodness to those surrounded by evil,
and love to the desperate of heart.
Your presence comes to challenge preconceived ideas,
topple the arrogant from their seat,
and to reveal to the rich the needs of the poor.*

*Deep within, my soul acknowledges in joy and praise
your love that is in this world.
Through your holy love, open the eyes of all
to seek the path of peace and righteousness. Amen*

John the Baptist

Reflective

During the weeks of Advent, we will be busily preparing for Christmas. There will be presents to wrap, the Christmas tree to decorate and the house to clean. There may also be the writing of lists of food to buy for the days leading up to and after Christmas, especially if family and friends are visiting. If all is to go smoothly, and as far as possible without stress, then preparation is important.

We also need to be preparing ourselves spiritually. As the days rush by, and the number of carol services increases, it's important to pause and be still with God in our own personal times of prayer. In this time of prayer we come before God, as God is about to be revealed in the incarnation.

John the Baptist was vocal in calling the people to repent and seek forgiveness, to be baptised, and to be prepared for the One to come. Out from the wilderness his voice echoes into our own lives, to seek forgiveness and to be prepared for the day that is soon to come.

Take time to reflect upon all the preparations still needed before Christmas comes. As you sit quietly in prayer, ask God to be with you in peace and that you will enjoy this time.

Take time to reflect upon the spiritual and prayerful preparations you can make by giving to God moments in each day to meet with him in prayer.

Baptism

Reflective

As the herald of the One who was to come, John the Baptist called the people to repent and to be baptised. He called them to be prepared for the coming of God's anointed One, to seek forgiveness and to enter into the waters of baptism.

For what do you feel you need to seek God's forgiveness? Bring it before him.

Do you remember your baptism? Often baptism takes place when we are a baby, and so we only know about it through the stories of those who were present.

In a time of prayer, imagine that you have come to be baptised, seeking forgiveness and a new life in Christ, promising to follow the way of Jesus, feeling the water being poured over your forehead, and being signed with the sign of the cross.

What feelings and thoughts come to you?

Baptism welcomes us into the family of God and calls us to enter into the Christian life. Through our growing faith we draw others to come and know God's love and presence.

With John the Baptist, we are called to prepare the way for others to come and know God. In the quietness of prayer, offer to God the ways in which you give witness to the faith you have, and ask how you can play your part in preparing the way of the Lord.

Help me, O God, to be bold in proclaiming you through the life I live.
Help me to feel the cleansing and renewing waters of baptism upon me,
the touch of the Spirit anointing me.
Help me to listen for your voice calling out to me, to 'prepare the way'.
Help me now, as you draw me closer to your coming upon earth,
not to be so busy that I forget to meet with you in quietness and in stillness.
Help me to seek refuge in the wilderness,
so I may truly be prepared through your presence and prayer in me,
to greet you anew on Christmas Day. Amen

Peace and light

Intercession

The words of Zechariah in the Gospel of Luke (1:67–80) bless the God who is active within creation. He speaks too of his

The season of Advent

son, declaring with prophetic words the way in which John will serve God and prepare the way for 'the Most High'. He looks back to his ancestors and the prophets of old, remembering their covenantal relationship with God. He looks forward to the coming dawn and light promised so long ago, that will guide all peoples in the way of peace.

In the rush of our Advent days, it's important to remember to look beyond our own personal prayer to offer prayers for peace in the wider world, to bring our words of prayer, hope and prophecy to God, the Most High.

As you begin this prayer of intercession for peace, spend some time quietly reflecting upon the places and people for which you feel you need to offer prayer. Take a map of the world and some small votive candles (or one larger candle) with you into your place of prayer. As you pray, light a votive candle and place it on the map for the area and people prayed for. Allow the light to bring peace to the area it touches.

If you don't have a world map, write on a large piece of paper the names of countries or people you will bring into prayer, and then place a lighted candle on each as you bring them to God in prayer.

At the end of the prayer, light another votive candle for yourself, asking God to be peace within you.

Where is God's peace and light needed in the world?
Where is God's peace and light needed in the church?
Where is God's peace and light needed in your community?
Where is God's peace and light needed in your home and family?
Where is God's peace and light needed in you?
How can you be a bearer of God's peace and light?

The love of God

Reflective

Read Song of Songs 8:6–7.

During the months of her pregnancy, Mary received the support of Joseph and Elizabeth. Her thoughts and emotions must have stretched between amazement and fear and a deep growing love for the child she carried and nurtured within her. With her own love, and the love of God upon her, this would be a love that gave her both courage and strength. This is a love that we too receive, a love that dwells within us, a love that allows us to return to God in faith.

When we look at the journey and life of Mary at this time, and the verses from the Song of Songs, we find love and passion; the desiring and passionate God. We discover too trust and commitment. Mary needed to commit herself in trust to God before she could bring God's child to birth. The lovers in the Song also needed to trust one another and be committed if they were to have their 'happy ending'.

To be able to open up ourselves and our lives to the caress of God's love, we need to be committed and prayerful in the faith we have, and to be able to trust ourselves to that love given to us. For some, it may be easy and comfortable to know that they are loved passionately by God; for others it may be difficult to accept or understand how much God loves them.

God is, however, a God of love. In that love he came in Jesus to be among us, and in the spirit to be eternally.

In a time of quiet prayer, reflect upon the love of God.

Slowly and prayerfully, read through the words in the passage from the Song of Songs. Which word or phrase seems important to you? What feelings does that word or phrase bring to you?

The season of Advent

Imagine God saying to you, 'I have set you as a seal upon my heart, set me as a seal upon your heart.' What thoughts and feelings come to you?

When you pray, what are the words you use when speaking to God? Do you, or could you, use words of love and desire, or refer to God in the feminine as well as, or instead of, the masculine?

Write your own prayer to God in your own words, and include the following.

- Your journey through these weeks of Advent
- Your thoughts about your faith and understanding (or not) of God
- Your feelings about God's love for you
- Your feelings about your love for God

Yours, O God, is a love of unimaginable depth,
unconditional and all-accepting.
Wash me in this love, cleanse me from all that hinders
and prevents me from loving you in return.
In that love, deepen my trust so, with Mary,
I may say, 'Here I am,'
to answer your call, to sow seeds of love with every step I take
every word I speak and every action I make.
In your love guide me towards the crib
of new life, new beginnings.
At the crib may I silently in my heart,
offer my love and myself in faith to you.
Come, O God, in and through
the struggles and pain of life,
bring to birth a deeper love in me
for you and all creation. Amen

7–20 DECEMBER

Taste and see

Sally Welch

Taste 1: Fasting

Bible reading

Read Genesis 3:1–13.

Traditionally, we use the season of Advent to prepare ourselves for the birth of Christ, trying not to restrict ourselves simply to the physical preparations necessary for the feast of Christmas, but to ready our hearts and minds to celebrate the coming of the Messiah into our sin-torn world. The following readings invite you to prepare for Advent using all your senses, your whole bodies in fact, and offer opportunities to respond in ways that help us focus once more on the message of love that is at the heart of the gospel.

We start this series where it all began, in the Garden of Eden, as Adam and Eve are faced with the most important choice of their lives. Adam and Eve choose to disobey God, and by doing so, set themselves apart from him. The course of humankind seems to be set on disaster. But even in the midst of tragedy, the seed of hope is present, and as the tale of the children of Israel begins, so too does God's plan for their redemption.

We too must make choices about how we will live our lives—whether we will believe in God's loving purposes for us or succumb to the temptation of doubt. Advent is a time for reassessing those choices and for reaffirming our determination to walk in God's ways.

Fasting was an expected discipline in both Old Testament and New Testament times, and this habit became an accepted part of personal spirituality for many Christians from Paul onwards. Although traditionally Lent has been the time for fasting, the season of Advent is known in the Eastern Orthodox church as the time of the 'nativity fast', as many people choose to abstain from food or luxuries as a way of preparation for Christmas. Why not consider giving up a favourite food or drink for a time, or changing an unprofitable use of time into a more constructive one? When undertaken in the right spirit, that of humility and prayer, such actions can remind us of our sins of pride and selfishness, and encourage a renewed dependence on God. Remember that fasting always goes hand in hand with prayer, so try also to set aside extra time for being with God.

Taste 2: Feast for Advent

Spotlight

Read Psalm 34.

The month of December can often seem a dark month in the northern hemisphere, with long nights and chilly days causing a feeling of bleakness which is compounded for some by a time of fasting, of abstinence from much-enjoyed treats. Two feast days serve to break up this austerity, providing moments of warmth and brightness to lighten the period of waiting which can seem so long-drawn-out.

On 6 December, the feast of St Nicolas is celebrated by many countries as enthusiastically as Christmas Day itself. Gifts for children may be left in shoes or stockings and spiced gingerbread is eaten. St Lucy, whose feast is on 13 December, is seen as a symbol of light, particularly appropriate for the long dark winters. A girl dressed in white and wearing a crown of candles

Taste and see

may lead processions, and *lussebullar* or saffron buns with raisins are shared by the community.

Both these feasts serve as a contrast to the surrounding days. Too often we take for granted the many blessings that we have, focusing instead on what we do not have. As we look forward to the birth of our Messiah in a situation of extreme poverty and desperation, we think of those who share this condition today.

All too often we disregard the good things that surround us, failing to appreciate them and taking them for granted. This exercise helps us to focus mindfully on the most basic of essentials—our food.

Take a piece of your favourite food. It can be sweet or savoury, but must be a luxury or something you particularly enjoy; a piece of chocolate is a good example. Begin by placing it on a plate in front of you, noticing its textures and colour, its shape and smell. Slowly put it in your mouth and allow its flavours to rest on your palate. Continue to eat with concentration, focusing on taste and texture, and the pleasure it brings. Thank God for his gifts of taste and smell, and for the plenty with which you are surrounded. Pray for those whose daily life is haunted by a lack of food.

Touch 1: The visit

Meditative

Read Luke 1:39–45.

Mary is young and frightened. She has been given a life-changing message by an angel—she is to bear the Son of God, to be the deliverer of redemption to the world. With one word of assent, she has changed the course of human history, but she is already becoming aware of the cost of this courageous deed. Her plans for her future came to the brink of collapse on

Joseph's realisation that she was pregnant. Seeking support, she journeys to see her cousin Elizabeth, who is also expecting a baby, although all had assumed that she was long past child-bearing age.

Elizabeth's reaction to Mary's arrival is everything Mary could have hoped for. Full of love, the cousins move to embrace each other and Elizabeth's swelling stomach bumps against Mary so that she too can feel the new life moving within the older woman's womb. Elizabeth is overjoyed to recognise that her cousin is the bearer of the Messiah, and her support and encouragement will be important to Mary in the months to come.

Touch is a powerful sense that is often underestimated. Those who live without the affectionate touch of others feel its lack contributing to their loneliness. As you prepare for Advent, try to remain aware of the ways you come into contact with others. Let your touch be supportive and meaningful, showing affection without becoming intrusive. Allow the tenderness you might feel for a newborn child to be reflected in your words and actions.

Touch 2: Rough and smooth

Bible reading

Read Luke 3:1–6.

My secondary school celebrated its quincentenary while I was in the sixth form, and we were delighted to be informed that the Queen would visit the school as part of the celebrations. Much time and effort was spent tidying up the grounds, cleaning some of the scruffier classrooms and redecorating the areas that the Queen would see. The excitement grew daily until the event itself, which was every bit as joyous as anticipated.

As John declares the coming of the Messiah, he invites us to join in with the created world in preparing for his arrival. Advent is a time for smoothing the rough, unfinished places of our lives, those areas that need forgiveness or healing, relationships that need resolving, situations that need clearing. Our hearts must be cleared of past resentments and grudges, our souls cleansed from sin, so that we may have space to welcome the bringer of love and light, and energy to share this love and light with those we meet.

Reflect on the difference between walking barefoot on rough, sharp pebbles and feeling smooth sand beneath our feet. You might like to find both these surfaces and walk barefoot on them. How much more focused can we be on the people and things that matter when we are not distracted by our own unease and discomfort! Pray for the grace to let go of the unnecessary and unhealthy in our lives, and embrace the smooth path of peace.

Sound 1: In the temple

Meditative

Read Luke 1:8–25.

Zechariah and Elizabeth are good people: they obey God's commandments and live good lives in God's sight. Sometimes, however, the very routine nature of their lives must have threatened to overwhelm them, as they struggled to deal with the major sorrow that was part of their relationship. Despite their prayers, God had not given them sons or daughters, and now Elizabeth was too old to have children.

This particular day, Zechariah has been chosen by lot to burn the incense on the altar, an important task which every priest aspired to. But the surprises of the day are not merely confined

Taste and see

to the significance of the job he is to do. An angel appears and announces the birth of a son to Elizabeth and Zechariah, whose effect upon the world will be cosmic; he will take his place in history as the one who prepares the children of Israel for the coming of the Messiah.

Zechariah does not really take much of this in, because his imagination has stopped at the first announcement of the angel: 'Your wife Elizabeth will bear you a son' (v. 13, NRSV). His response is total disbelief. Years of obedience, discipline and prayer fall away, and all Zechariah can do is protest to this heavenly being that what is being announced is impossible. For this Zechariah is silenced.

Sometimes we don't listen to God because we don't want to hear what he is saying to us. Sometimes our preoccupation with the routine of daily existence drowns out the still small voice of God. Advent is a time for silence, for making space to hear the good news, for shutting out the noise and clamour so that we can hear the whisper of love.

Practise being silent for a period of time each day. It may be for only a few minutes, depending on the time you have available. You may find it helpful to write down your reactions to silence and any insights received.

Sound 2: Advent carols

Spotlight/creative

Read Luke 1:46–55.

By the middle of December, it will be almost impossible to escape the sound of Christmas carols and songs. It is easy to become irritated by this sudden immersion in Christmas music, but singing is one of the most ancient of impulses, and the urge to set words to music, to express emotions in melody and tune, is universal.

Singing makes us breathe deeply, steadying our heart rate. Singing boosts our immune system, reduces stress levels and, according to scientists, helps us to bear chronic pain better. It is better for your health than yoga and, according to one study in the USA, even increases life expectancy.

Albert van den Heuvel of the World Council of Churches goes even further. 'It is the hymns repeated over and over again which form the container of much of our faith. They are probably in our age the only confessional documents which we learn by heart. As such they have taken the place of our catechisms... Tell me what you sing, and I'll tell you who you are' (*New Hymns for a New Day*, World Council of Churches, Geneva, 1966).

It seems totally appropriate, therefore, that the event that will change all time for ever is heralded by a song. In her joyful response, Mary moves beyond prose, beyond the ordinary and the everyday to herald the extraordinary goodness of God, and in doing so, promises that the Messiah will break into our own ordinary worlds to meet us in our everyday activities, joys and challenges.

During the weeks of Advent, try to increase the amount you sing. You do not need to join a choir, although you might wish to; you could simply sing as you journey to work or when you are at home. Go for a walk in the country and sing carols as loudly as you can. Best of all, find an event or carol service and join with others in celebrating the imminent arrival of the one whose love transforms our own meagre sound offerings into music worthy of angels.

Taste and see

Smell 1: Cooking

Creative

Read Hosea 14:4–7.

Some of the most moving and inspiring passages of the Old Testament occur when the writers look forward to the birth of the Messiah, the Redeemer, the one who will make whole once more this sin-damaged world. These passages are rich in metaphors and use all five senses to give us a heightened sense of the glory of God and something of the excitement of the anticipation we feel as the nativity event approaches. Some of the expressions are unusual, encouraging us to look at the event in a new way, bringing a new dimension to a potentially overfamiliar story.

Writers remembering childhood Christmases often highlight the scents and smells of the festival, recalling the heady mixture of pine and fir decorations mingled with spices such as cinnamon and cloves to produce an aroma that filled the entire house and contributed to the excitement of anticipation. In a similar way Old Testament writers evoke the scents of the cedar trees of Lebanon, of apples, vines, perfume and incense to provide an aromatic picture of delights to come.

Bring the scents of Christmas into your home by baking. The smell of a freshly cooked sponge or fruit cake or the spiciness of gingerbread cookies will lift the spirits of those who come into your home, and you will have something to offer them! If you do not have easy access to cooking facilities, try making a cake in a mug. Simply mix four tablespoonfuls of self-raising flour with four tablespoons of sugar and two of cocoa powder together in a large microwaveable mug. Add one egg and mix it well, then pour in three tablespoonfuls of sunflower oil and three tablespoonfuls of milk. Mix the whole lot together thoroughly, then microwave for between three and five minutes.

Alternatively, try boiling some water in a pan and adding powdered cinnamon and cloves. The scented steam will soon fill the room with the fragrance of anticipation!

Smell 2: Incense

Prayer

Read Psalm 141.

Our sense of smell is connected to the part of our brains that deals with our emotions and is strongly linked to our memories. This is why scents such as newly mown grass can produce such powerful memories of childhood, or why a scent associated with a particular event can give us instant reminders of that time.

We can use our sense of smell in our prayers to recall the blessings of the past and to look to the future.

Light a scented candle and allow a few minutes for it to burn and the scent to fill the room.

Loving God, as the scent of this candle mingles with the smoke rising before us, we bring before you our whole selves; hearts, minds and bodies given in praise of your greatness. We remember your sacrifice for us in the form of your Son, whose arrival we await with eager anticipation, and we ask for your grace to fill us as we prepare for his coming.

Generous God, we thank you for the gifts and blessings we have received from your hands through the years. We remember with gratitude the moments of loving kindness we have shared and the glimpses of your saving love in the actions and words of those around us. We pledge ourselves to sharing your love with those who share our lives, in your name.

Compassionate God, we bring before you those whose memories are bleak and painful, those who have suffered damage at the hands of those closest to them, victims of abuse and neglect. Heal their wounds and cleanse them of their sorrow, that they might look forward to your coming with anticipation of love.

Glorious God, the arrival of your Son was heralded by angels; let us act as your heralds in the world, bringing the news of your healing love into this world which so desperately seeks to be made whole once more. Amen

Sight 1: Light

Creative

Read Luke 1:67–80.

The image of Jesus as not only bringing light to the world but being the source of that very light is tremendously powerful. The love of God in Christ shines into the darkness of sorrow and suffering, bringing healing and love. It is of this love that Zechariah sings when his tongue is finally loosened at the birth of his son John, who in his turn will foretell of the saving love of God brought into the world in the person of Christ. Even though Zechariah does not yet know how this will happen, he trusts in God's love and looks forward with faith to a light-filled future.

There are times in our lives when the darkness threatens to overwhelm us, when we find it hard to believe in the light and love of Christ. In the shadowy time of Advent, we look forward to the time of light and love, even though it may seem to us that this light is far off.

There is a prayer which was reputedly found scratched on a wall of a prison cell in Cologne during World War II.

I believe in the sun, even when it does not shine.
I believe in love, even when I cannot feel it.
I believe in God, even when he is silent.

Make a collage of people or situations you wish to pray for, using pictures or photographs from newspapers and magazines. If you have an old box about the size of a shoebox, you can line the inside of the box with these pictures for a more powerful effect. Cut out two holes in the box, one in the lid and one in one side. Shine the light of torch through the hole in the top of the box and look through the hole in the side. Allow the light of the torch to play on different parts of the collage and pray for each situation, that it may experience the light of Christ.

Sight 2: Christingle

Spotlight

Read John 1:1–14.

The Christingle has become a familiar sight in schools and churches in recent years during the Advent and Christmas seasons.

It is believed that the Christingle originally came to us from the Moravian church, whose congregations traditionally brought gifts for the poorer members of their communities. One pastor was in the habit of giving a candle in return as a reminder to children that Jesus was the light of the world. This candle was pushed into the top of an orange both to increase stability and also as a gift for the child. Over the years, this custom spread and more features were added to the Christingle or 'Christ Light'. The orange was held to represent the world, with a bright red ribbon tied around it as a reminder of Christ's blood, shed for all. The four cocktail sticks pushed in at various angles near the top of the orange are the four seasons, and the sweet things they carry represent the gifts of each season.

Today in the UK, the Christingle carries a further symbolism in that the money collected at a Christingle service is usually given to the Children's Society, linking back to its origins as an opportunity to share the plenty of one group of people with those who are not so fortunate.

You might wish to find a Christingle service in your neighbourhood and attend it, praying for the families and children who gather to hear the Christmas story together. If you can, bring a Christingle home and place it where its light can be seen by others. In the early mornings or evenings of Advent, the candle can be lit and prayers said for children everywhere. Or you could make a Christingle yourself and use it as a focus for your prayers for the world.

Our whole selves dancing

Bible reading/creative

Read 2 Samuel 6:1–14.

For many years, the ark of the covenant had been absent from the children of Israel. That precious container of the ten commandments was a symbol of God's ongoing loving care for them, a reminder of all that he had done in their lives and a promise of all that he would continue to do. Because of the actions of Saul, the ark had been captured by the Philistines, and the core of the Israelites' worship was hollow. But now David was king and he had transformed the fortunes of Israel. After many successful military campaigns he had returned the land of Israel to its people and restored the city of Jerusalem to them. Now, at last, the ark is coming home.

David goes out to meet the ark as it proceeds triumphantly through the city gates, and so great is his delight that he dances. He dances because he is on the edge of mystery; he dances because his heart is so full that he can find no other expression for the way he feels but through the whole of his being. Used to living in the hinterlands of danger, his life constantly at risk, he knows he needs God, and he honours this with his whole being.

In our approach to Advent, let us bring our whole selves before God in our worship, putting aside all reticence and preconceived ideas about what is appropriate behaviour, and let us look forward to the coming of the Saviour with the same joy that David heralded the entry of the ark of the covenant, God's promise, into Jerusalem.

Practise praising God with your whole body. Try putting on your favourite religious music, whether this is hymns, contemporary songs or classical music, and move to the rhythms you hear. Let your love for God fill your whole body so that you lose self-consciousness and allow praise to flow from you.

Our whole selves moulding

Creative

Read Isaiah 64:1–9.

As Isaiah looks forward to the coming of the Messiah, he reminds us that one of the common mistakes we make is to try to tell God what he should be doing! Too often in our prayers and intercessions we provide him with a list of instructions and advice on how he could order his universe in a better way, or at least in a way more convenient for us. In this passage Isaiah admonishes us for our arrogance in assuming that we know better than our creator what is best for us. He reminds us that we are created by an all-powerful, all-loving God who holds our lives tenderly in his hands. He moulded us and shaped us; he has a purpose for which he designed us and which only we can accomplish. We must pray for insight to discern God's purposes for us in this world and for the grace to fulfil them. Above all, let us trust in God's redeeming love as shown to us in Jesus.

Buy a small pot of children's play dough or mix half a cup of domestic salt with a cup of flour in a bowl. Slowly mix in half a cup of water until the dough is soft and pliable but not sticky.

Use the dough in your prayer time, gently moulding it and shaping it. Remind yourself that God created you with love, that he fashioned you for his purposes, and ask God to reveal those purposes to you.

Creator God, you made us and gave us life, breathing your loving Spirit into each one of us. Help us during this Advent season to prepare for your coming into the world. Help us to direct our lives to your ways and to fulfil the purposes you have for us. Amen

21 DECEMBER–3 JANUARY

Joseph, unsung Christmas hero

Janet Lunt

Introduction

Visual

There has always been a large place in my heart for Joseph, adoptive parent of Jesus. References to him in the Gospels are underwhelming considering the closeness he had to Jesus for many years. Although he is named as a saint, his titles can seem underplayed if not subordinate, as he is often referred to as 'husband of Mary' or 'Joseph the worker', patron saint of carpenters and labourers. The Greek Gospels describe him as a *tekton*, a word commonly used for a craftsman or artisan, often a carpenter or builder, someone working with their hands, in wood, iron or stone. It appears he taught his craft to Jesus, who is also referred to as a *tekton* in Mark 6:3.

Joseph is mentioned only a few times in the Gospels, yet those brief glimpses reveal him as a kingpin in God's plan for salvation and hugely significant in Jesus' upbringing. Scholars assume he died before Christ's ministry began, for Joseph disappeared from the Gospel writers' radar after the incident of losing the twelve-year-old Jesus and later finding him in his heavenly Father's house (Luke 2:41–52). Perhaps this is why he is often overlooked.

You are invited to walk alongside Joseph through the Christmas narrative and beyond, gleaning fresh insights from his brief appearances in the Gospels.

Bring to mind your own recollections of Joseph. Search for pictures which include Joseph, in art books, on the internet, or among your Christmas cards. How is he portrayed? What is he doing in the pictures? Perhaps use a Christmas card depicting Joseph as your bookmark for the next two weeks. Ask the Lord to bring to life once again the drama that is Christmas, making it meaningful to your life in a new way.

All change

Bible reflection

Think of a time when you were badly let down, recollecting how you felt and acted. Were you tempted to retaliate, spread your story of hurt?

How might you react to a daughter, friend or partner announcing she is miraculously pregnant through God's doing?

We don't know who broke the news to Joseph nor how much he was told, but imagine his inner turmoil when he discovered Mary was carrying someone else's child. Read his initial reactions in Matthew 1:18–20. He was looking forward to his marriage, grateful for a wife who reverenced the God of Israel, only to find his dream shattered by apparent unfaithfulness. Any explanation would sound incredible, adding insult to injury (even Mary questioned Gabriel how it was possible). The news must have stung badly. Severing the marriage agreement would have been expected; unfaithfulness damages relationships. Everything had changed.

However, notice how Joseph is described. The text indicates a caring man who thought before he acted. Joseph, who adhered to Judaic law, was also merciful. Public shaming could mean Mary would become an outcast and could even be stoned.

Whatever shock, indignation or sorrow Joseph experienced, he showed self-control and concern rather than seeking pity or revenge. Verses 24–25 show his embrace of the world-changing nativity. God's long-desired plan balanced momentarily on a precipice. Although the Lord knew Joseph's heart, there was a calculated risk involved—the risk of scripture not being fulfilled, Mary being shamed as a single parent, Jesus not being born in Bethlehem. God didn't reprimand Joseph for his initial intentions. The angel told him not to fear, explained, and sought cooperation for the new thing God was doing.

God chose to seek human cooperation, with all the risk it entailed. How do you feel about God's desire for your cooperation and involvement in his plans?

Read the prophetic verses from Isaiah 43:18–19. The metaphors from nature richly illustrate God's desire to regain the hearts of his people and restore relationship. Give thanks for their fulfilment in Jesus Christ. Perhaps these verses have something to say today, to the church, to you. Allow time for them to speak to you.

Adopting God's plan

Creative

Read Matthew 1:18–25.

While Joseph was still considering what to do, God came to him. Divine intervention was crucial for Joseph, because the new thing God wanted to do was ground-breaking in the extreme. Joseph immediately recognised that his experience was not just a vivid dream but angelic, exacting, compelling. This indicates a man who practised his faith and desired to do God's

Joseph, unsung Christmas hero

will, a person awaiting the Messiah.

If Zechariah and Elisabeth were chosen to rear John the Baptist because they were blameless and righteous before God (implied in Luke 1:6), it follows that both Mary and Joseph were chosen for similar qualities, able to provide a home environment in which the young Messiah could be nurtured. They were set apart, consecrated (the meaning of 'holy'), to enable the young Christ to develop and prepare for ministry.

Joseph believed, obeyed and took responsibility—without question. Taking the angel at his word, he said 'yes' to God. The calling delivered to both Joseph and Mary by angels would bind them together for the difficult and dangerous path ahead as they lived in humble obedience to God's direction. Joseph adopted God's Son unquestioningly, although, no doubt, he felt overwhelmed at times by this responsibility.

What do you have in common with Joseph? Recollect life-changing points on your journey with God when you made a public commitment to Christ or felt called to take on a special role in his name.

In the Magnificat (Luke 1:46–55), Mary poured out words of joy, hope and praise because the Lord had chosen her. The fulfilment of God's word prompted Zechariah to utter eloquent praise and prophecy when his speech returned on the birth of John the Baptist (vv. 67–79). What might Joseph have expressed after being invited by the angel to participate in God's revelation? Compose a fitting 'Joseph benediction' or prayer response, or create a prayer-poem about Joseph, commending him and thanking God for his example.

A long dark night

Imaginative/prayer

How rough this road to Bethlehem is! I hadn't noticed before, but with Mary in the throes of labour, uncomfortable on the donkey, I am aware of every stone. She doesn't complain but must feel anxious, so far from home. Night is approaching. It's already dark enough to see the first stars, and there's that new bright one again.

This journey seems to be taking for ever. I fear Mary will have to give birth by the roadside! Even for the practised, birth is an anxious prospect. Worse, if I can't find a midwife in Bethlehem, I will have to deliver the child myself! It feels like bad timing, the baby due and the census taking place. But then, it's God's baby, so I have to trust him with the timing.

What if I fail, though? What if the child dies? This is the greatest responsibility I've ever had to shoulder. Courage, my soul! Be strong for Mary's sake. I will remind myself of Zechariah and Elizabeth's miracle baby, delivered safely, despite their age—and what stories circulate because Zechariah was struck dumb by his vision, then suddenly could speak at the moment of naming the child! Neighbours are awestruck, saying God is on the move.

At last. We arrive at the gates, but what a crowd! Here for the census, I guess. I must find a room quickly, and a midwife… Another queue… Another full inn… Where else can I try? My feet are blistered. Poor Mary, she is struggling. I will cry out like my ancestor David: Where are you, Lord? Hear my prayer! When will this night end? Everyone needs a bed tonight, and no innkeeper wants a birth in their overcrowded tavern, but this is your son Jesus (yes, the meaningful name I must give to him).

At first, I want to refuse this meagre stable, but Mary can't go on. Is this really part of God's plan? The shame of the place, the smell. Will my wife feel I have failed in her hour of need? I thought this moment would be glorious, special, but it is as risky as any other baby coming into the world. Be still, my soul. God's will be done… Not long now, Mary… not long…

Waiting in the darkness or with the unknown is hard. Prayer requests may remain unanswered; God may seem absent. Light a candle, and wait for a while in quietness and expectant hope. Close with the following (or your own) prayer.

Lord, Joseph could not see what lay ahead,
and may have doubted your love in the long, dark night
but he kept going on his journey.
Joseph may have feared you had deserted him
but he kept on knocking until a door opened.

Lord, when I cannot see what lies ahead
or face the dark, the unknown
help me to keep going on my journey.
When I doubt or fear, when doors are closed to me
help me to keep on knocking, trusting,
until I see your will come to birth
on earth as it is in heaven. Amen

New arrival

Creative

The birth of a new baby is life-changing. Demands become full on with feeding, nappies and attempts to respond to the cries of one who cannot explain him- or herself. Nights are broken. It is

Joseph, unsung Christmas hero

a daunting task, following swiftly on from an always risky birth experience. People visit; cards arrive; special presents are given to acknowledge the wonder.

Joseph and Mary experienced visitors and gifts, but not the usual ones. Under a borrowed roof in a strange town, amid animals and fodder, grubby shepherds became substitutes for friends and family, and congratulations were laced with supernatural stories of singing angels. No doubt Joseph and Mary experienced the usual anxieties on the arrival of Jesus, and had no grandparents on hand to advise them.

Jesus was safely delivered. For both Joseph and Mary, it was not only life-changing to experience a first baby, but more, it was life-changing for their journey with God, for after the long, long night confirmation abounded that God was watching over it all, reminding the new parents that it wasn't all a strange dream.

What went through Joseph's mind as he looked upon this tiny, vulnerable life asleep in the hay, needing protection and nurture for years to come? Would they be up to the task of parenting Jesus? Perhaps in a quiet moment after the birth, Joseph gave thanks to God that the first task was safely over, the nativity of God's child.

Create a 'new arrival' card for Jesus. Draw or collage a picture on the front. Write your own words of greeting inside. You could tell him he is welcome in your heart and home, even though Bethlehem could only provide a manger.

Visualise entering the stable, giving your card to the new mother, then standing by the new father to see baby Jesus.

Joseph, unsung Christmas hero

To our small planet

Going outside/meditative

If possible, do this meditation outside when it's dark; you will need a Bible and torch. If you are indoors, look for images of the universe, available on the internet.

You sit or stand outside under a clear night sky, as Joseph might have done, holding the new baby while Mary slept. Did he contemplate the myriad of silent, shimmering stars, or hear the faint sound of harmonised singing? You allow peace to descend, and marvel at the miracle of God coming to earth.

You visualise earth, a sapphire-blue globe, with its little white moon, spinning as it orbits our essential giant sun… and the companion planets of our solar system, noticing that our world is much smaller than the gas giants of Jupiter, Saturn, Uranus, Neptune, yet larger than Mercury, Mars and Venus; each one far away and uniquely different in size, colour and moons. You wonder at our world suspended like a jewel in space, its life-giving, fluffy white clouds swirling in marbled patterns over land masses and oceans. It teems with creatures, yet from a distance none is visible at all. You consider earth's position, perfectly placed for life to flourish, noting that our sun-system is but a speck in one arm of a radiant spiral galaxy of solar systems, our sun one of the smaller stars among the billions of this Milky Way and 27,000 light years from its centre. You try to grasp that the Milky Way, in turn, is a small rotating galaxy in a gigantic, expansive, infinite cosmos of galaxies and star-nurseries.

You say with the psalmist: 'When I consider your heavens, the work of your fingers, the moon and stars which you have set in place, what is humankind that you are mindful of them, human beings that you care for them? You have made them a little lower than the angels and crowned them with glory and honour' (Psalm 8:3–5, NIV).

Why, in this vast universe, should God visit our tiny world in his Son, whom we hosted so badly? Jesus, who lived for three decades with Joseph and Mary, walked in the dust, made things from wood, laughed and cried, felt passion and pain, spoke Aramaic, Hebrew and possibly Greek. He changed lives with his touch, actions, words. His death could not prevent God's winning love breaking through in unstoppable resurrection-life, life for all. You are part of this extraordinary love story, beginning with Christ's birth. Marvelling at the vastness and intimacy of God, celebrate your spiritual nativity, and offer worship to your Creator-Rescuer.

Journeying into the unknown

Creative/reflective

Joseph was a hard-working carpenter who observed Jewish religious customs. He had planned a marriage, hoping for sons to learn his trade; like all of Israel he would be living in hope of liberation from the occupying Romans. Then, quite suddenly, he was asked to set out on a dangerous, selfless journey of faith, completely reliant on God's direction. On the way, he discovered that others were also being asked to step out into the unknown with God: Mary (Luke 1:30–32); her cousin Elizabeth and Zechariah and their son John (vv. 13–16); sages (Matthew 2:1–12) and shepherds (Luke 2:8–20); Simeon and Anna (vv. 22–38). Each person was invited to participate in the labour pains of the new, unknown kingdom, some simply as witnesses sharing heaven's rejoicing, others playing a larger part protecting and preparing the way for the ministry of God's Son. Although Joseph's role was unique (Matthew 1:20–22), he found he was not alone.

Joseph, unsung Christmas hero

Joseph heard the story of simple shepherds whose spirits were awakened through an extraordinary experience of angels giving directions to find their Saviour and a taste of heaven's worship. Then, from the mysterious eastern strangers, he discovered that God's reach extended beyond his own imagination and borders, that their search for God's revelation required a momentous journey abroad employing their knowledge, wealth and ability to travel. He observed in Simeon and Anna the fulfilment of years of faithful prayer attuned to the Holy Spirit. Joseph must have found God's ways mind-stretching and life-defining.

Have you come to God after a long search like the wise men—a costly, painstaking and thoughtful process? Or were you surprised and convinced quite suddenly, like the shepherds? Perhaps you identify more with Joseph, or another of the characters mentioned above, those waiting in prayer or those asked to sacrifice normality.

Draw a crazy-paving path to represent your journey of faith so far. Write individual items or names in each space: those in scripture whose lives have increased your faith; those who have inspired or helped you, from history, and now; books that opened your eyes, difficulties that bore fruit, events, and so on. Create a colour-key for each category and fill or outline each shape accordingly. Thank God for the company of heaven who aid your journey into the unknown.

A star overhead

Visual/creative

This year, I have been given a wonderful bucket-list gift of a telescope. Learning to use it is a steep learning curve. I am amazed to discover that what we see of Saturn takes two days to reach us. We can see and know so much more now than people could in Jesus' day, yet the universe still holds endless mysteries.

Two thousand years ago, people believed that a new celestial body in the night sky was a sign. The sages believed, more specifically, that the star heralded the birth of a divine king, and were compelled to seek him. Each night, the star rose in its circuit, indicating roughly where the gifted arrival would be, but a distant star can't really pinpoint a house. Eventually, with help from Herod's advisers and perhaps from Bethlehem locals, they located Jesus beneath his star and were overjoyed. Assuming from their court visit that the strangers spoke a recognisable language, they probably informed Joseph and Mary of the star, possibly pointing it out. I wonder what effect knowledge of the new star had upon the parents, secretly indicating the child's whereabouts to those to whom God revealed it?

Although it seems fanciful, imagine that God created a special star to mark your birth and your unique role on earth. Is there an idea or spark of a dream, like a distant star, beckoning you to bring to birth something extraordinary for Christ? Talk with God about any faint glimmer of inspiration, ideas or dreams, asking for clarity. To remind yourself of these things, you could make a decorative star, and put it away with the decorations at the end of the season, observing any developments in your life next Christmas.

Time of angels

Creative

During that first Christmas, there was a concentration of angelic appearances. Many people are at ease with the idea of angels through carols, familiar readings and artworks, and angels are often viewed as beautiful, benign creatures that sometimes invisibly guard us from accidents. But let's pause for a moment. Is that the true picture? Experiences of them in the Bible are varied. Some came in human form, some in vivid dreams as with Joseph and the wise men, giving supernatural instruction. Zechariah was reprimanded and temporarily silenced by the angel Gabriel for questioning the message the angel brought. Jesus experienced an angel in Gethsemane to strengthen him (Luke 22:43), and two were involved in the resurrection (24:4). An angel with a sword, captain of the heavenly army, appeared to Joshua (Joshua 5:13–65).

Biblically, a visit from an angel generally meant that an individual needed help or encouragement, or instructions because something important was going to happen. Their presence could be, one assumes, quite frightening, for they often opened with: 'Don't be afraid.' Angels were and are God's messengers, and therefore embodiments of God's voice. People today claim to experience them, often in a saving capacity. For me, the experience to covet would be that of the shepherds, seeing and hearing a host of angels praising God.

What do you think about God's angels? To aid your thoughts, you could play some music that you consider to be like angels singing, and look at various representations of them in art.

To Egypt and back again

Intercession

Find a map of the Holy Land and Egypt, and trace the journeys Joseph navigated with his family: from Nazareth to Bethlehem, on to Egypt, back to settle in Nazareth and, somewhere in between, two visits to Jerusalem for Jesus' circumcision on the eighth day, and Mary's purification after 40 days (probably from Bethlehem).

Their journeys would be mostly on foot, sometimes with a donkey. It is roughly 80 miles from Nazareth to Bethlehem, 5½ miles from Bethlehem to Jerusalem, and approximately 350 miles from Bethlehem to the Egyptian Delta. It was common, and safer, to travel in groups (caravans) to avoid wild beasts and bandits. Joseph and Mary probably travelled to Bethlehem for the census with a group from their area. But was their hasty journey to Egypt done alone or not? It is most likely that the family fled to Egypt's Nile Delta following the caravan route along the coast of the Sinai Peninsula where there were inns and watering holes, rather than through the hot, uninhabitable Sinai desert. The holy family had become refugees (Matthew 2:13–23).

Pray for today's refugees and lands troubled by war and religious controversy. Remember everyone involved: the hurt, those who inflict hurt, the politicians, the powerless. Joseph was not exempt from struggle and threat, but God was with him, shaping the plan of salvation and showing him the way through for his vulnerable family.

The hidden story

Bible reading

Joseph waited in Egypt until God indicated the time to return to Israel (Matthew 2:19–23). They settled back in Nazareth and the story goes almost completely silent until God's Son emerges for ministry. Joseph returned to carpentry. The true identity of Jesus was kept hidden, and life became seemingly normal—implied in the later account when Jesus teaches in Nazareth's synagogue and locals consider the family too ordinary to produce a prophet (13:53–58).

Joseph would continue to protect the boy through childhood, spending time with him, teaching him his skills. Like other Jewish fathers of the time, he would teach Jesus what he knew of Judaism and the Torah, and perhaps Hebrew. Both parents would be very influential in Jesus' development, and we know they did a good job because 'the child grew and became strong; he was filled with wisdom, and the grace of God was on him' (Luke 2:40, NIV). It seems that they went on to have several children (Matthew 13:55–56), and Jesus grew up relating to his siblings, gaining all-important insights into human nature.

But could life in their house be truly normal, after the angelic intervention and upheavals of those early years? Was it like having a prodigy for a child? Did God have to warn Joseph often of imminent dangers? At some point before the first recorded miracle, did Jesus perform miracles at home? Mary was very sure at the Cana wedding that he could save the day (John 2:3).

Read Luke 2:41–52. On this occasion we are given a glimpse of the self-awareness and sense of calling that the adolescent Jesus possessed, aged only twelve; and more, he called God his 'Father', an unknown form of address at the time. Joseph and Mary couldn't understand what he was saying. Although Jesus obediently conformed to their concerns after this event, it must have been a watershed moment for his parents. Did Joseph see the need to decrease his fathering to leave more room for the Heavenly Father? One thing is certain; the whole of his relationship with Jesus required an open heart.

Imagine Joseph in his fatherly role with the young Jesus, perhaps telling him about the angels and the star surrounding his birth.

Joseph, a person to emulate

Reflective

If only we knew more about Joseph! However, the New Testament reveals many of his qualities. Joseph was serious about his faith, caring and thoughtful, self-controlled and merciful. He was a willing background support, a servant of God. He had 'ears to hear' and his obedience was exemplary. Joseph acted upon God's word without question, although not much is made of this. Mary and Zechariah had questions when Gabriel visited them, Zechariah earning quite a tabloid splash in the scriptures. Perhaps Joseph was unassuming, easily overlooked; but I doubt not that this good and devoted man pleased God. Joseph would truly be someone to emulate. How has he inspired you?

How do you imagine God greeted Joseph when he died? If you could rename him as a saint (and wished to), what appropriate title would you choose? (For example, St Joseph the Listener.) Or you could think of a symbol for him.

The epic story Joseph was drawn into continues, and we are today's witnesses of heaven come to earth, bearers of God-with-us and tellers of the story. As you look ahead in this new year, what new resolution might you make about your part in the greatest and unfinished story of love?

As a Child

Phil Steer

Believed

> *Yet to all who received him, to those who* believed *in his name, he gave the right to become children of God.*
> JOHN 1:12, NIV 1984, EMPHASIS MINE

In the book *Alice Through The Looking Glass* by Lewis Carroll there is a short exchange between Alice and the White Queen on the subject of belief. 'I can't believe that!' says Alice, responding to the White Queen's claim that she is 'one hundred and one, five months and a day', 'one can't believe impossible things.' 'I daresay you haven't had much practice,' says the Queen. 'Why, sometimes I've believed as many as six impossible things before breakfast.'

As Christians, many of us will have experienced periods of doubt during which it can feel as if holding on to our faith requires just such mental gymnastics. And if this is how it can sometimes seem for those who have seen at least something of the reality of God and his kingdom in our lives, just consider for a moment how hard belief must be for those who have not seen, and with whom we seek to share the good news of Jesus.

Indeed, I well remember when, in my late teens, I first began thinking about the meaning of 'Life, the Universe and Everything' (as the writer Douglas Adams would have it), and discussing spiritual matters with a few school friends who happened to go to church. My reaction at the time was just the same as Alice's: 'one can't believe impossible things'—or, as I stated emphatically, 'I can't make myself believe what I don't believe!'

Let's be honest, such a reaction is not altogether surprising: Jesus as both man and God, his birth to a virgin, his miracles and healings, his perfect and sinless life, his rising from the dead, indeed the very existence of God himself—there, that's 'six impossible things' for starters! Then there's the explanation of why Jesus' life and death was necessary and what it all achieved: our rebellion against God, our fall from grace, the broken relationship, the need for justice, the perfect sacrifice, the price paid, death defeated, complete forgiveness, eternal life. It's a lot for someone to get their head around.

And yet I can't help but wonder if we don't have a tendency to overcomplicate things. A few years ago a British bank ran an advertising campaign which focused on their claim that they provided simple and straightforward services, 'because life's complicated enough'. I can almost imagine Jesus making the same claim for the good news of his kingdom; this too is meant to be simple and straightforward—so simple and straightforward in fact that a little child can accept it. Indeed, not only can a little child accept it, but only a little child can accept it: for as Jesus says, 'anyone who will not receive the kingdom of God like a little child will never enter it' (Mark 10:15).

But let's be honest, most young children would seem to have little or no concept of what the good news of the kingdom is really all about; and this being the case, how can they possibly accept something they don't understand? The obvious answer is that they don't really accept it at all, they just blindly believe whatever they are told—and that therefore their belief in God is really no different from their belief in, say, Father Christmas or the Tooth Fairy.

While there is undoubtedly some truth in this, it would be wrong to conclude that this somehow invalidates a little child's acceptance of God and his kingdom. The authenticity of their childlike faith rests upon the reality of God, not upon the depth of their understanding.

We all too readily reduce the good news to a set of statements to be believed, a series of assertions to be accepted; but this is not what it is meant to be at all. Indeed, much of the message that we feel we have to communicate is not, in fact, an integral part of the good news of Jesus. Rather, it comes in large part from the New Testament letters and, as such, was written not to explain the faith to non-believers, but to help the members of the early Church understand what they had already accepted. It was written, in other words, to encourage those who already had a faith in Jesus, not to convince those who did not.

None of which is to suggest that what we believe about the good news is unimportant, or that you have to abandon your intellect and understanding and leave your brain behind when you become a Christian. But intellectual knowledge is not the key to the kingdom; indeed, I suspect that very few people are actually convinced into a belief that the good news is true.

Some years back I was involved in leading the Alpha course that our church put on for people wanting to explore the Christian faith. As we prepared for one course, the phrase 'taste and see that the Lord is good' (Psalm 34:8) came to mind. Our sense was very much that people would come to faith not so much through what was said in the talks, or through having their questions answered during the discussions afterwards, but through seeing and experiencing the reality of God in their own lives and in the lives of others involved with the course.

I committed my life to God while still not truly believing any of the 'impossible things' that had seemed such a stumbling block to my coming to faith. As I had argued with my friends, I had indeed been unable to make myself believe what I didn't believe. But I had got to the point (or rather, as I see now, God had brought me to the point) where I was able to accept that it might just possibly be true—and, if so, I ought to do something about it. And so, still unbelieving, I prayed to this God who might not exist, and offered my life to him if he did. At the time I felt no different. But the next day, speaking of what I had done, I was suddenly filled with an assurance that it was indeed true. For me, this was my personal experience of Paul's promise to the church in Corinth: 'Now it is God who makes both us and you stand firm in Christ. He anointed us, set his seal of ownership on us, and put his Spirit in our hearts as a deposit, guaranteeing what is to come' (2 Corinthians 1:21–22).

It would be wrong, of course, to build a theology on one's own personal experiences; nonetheless, I do think this illustrates an important point. We tend to feel that people will not come to faith unless they truly believe the good news of Jesus, having arrived at a conviction and a confidence that it is true. But a belief such as this is not, primarily, the result of human reasoning: it is the work of God's Holy Spirit in a person's life. Rather than being a precondition of commitment, frequently it comes only after a person has chosen to give their life to God.

For we are called not to believe a doctrine, but to believe in Jesus. It is a belief, not in something, but in someone. It is like a people believing in their President, or an army believing in its commander. Perhaps more pertinently, it is like a child believing in her parents, believing that they are in control, that they know what is best and will look after her. It is not so much a head-knowledge as a heart-response. It is saying to Jesus, 'I will put my trust in you, and seek to follow where you lead.'

Spotlight: Julian Meetings

Deidre Morris, GB Coordinator for Julian Meetings

Julian Meetings are quiet spaces where we can seek God in stillness and silence. They are ecumenical groups that have been meeting regularly over the last 40 years for contemplative prayer in the Christian tradition.

Contemplative prayer is like sitting before a painting and just looking at it—not studying it to see how it was painted, what the subject matter is or how the artist portrayed it (all this would be meditation) but simply looking at the painting and letting it 'speak' in whatever way it might. So in contemplation we just 'are' before God with the four 'S's: Stillness, Silence, Simplicity and Surrender.

Stillness enables us to give all our attention to God. It is most important when a group contemplates, as movement or noise from one person can be a distraction to others.

Silence allows for the 'still, small voice' of God to be heard, and helps us to focus our attention on God—not easy in a society where noise is used as an escape.

Simplicity does not mean it is easy, but that it needs minimal external input.

Surrender—much of our Christian life (when, where and how we pray, worship, study) is decided by us. In contemplation we give all the initiative to God, letting God be in control, not us.

Stillness and silence help us to *be*, fully in the present moment, entirely aware of *now*. Julian Meetings allow us to experience being with God in stillness and silence, but with a group of other people. This is quite different from contemplating alone. There is a depth to this 'gathered silence' which is impossible to explain—it can only be experienced.

At a Julian Meeting, held in a house, church or chapel, the members usually sit in a circle, often with a lit candle or other visual focus in the centre. One person leads into the silence, keeps track of time, and leads out of the silence after 30, 45, 60 minutes, however long the group chooses. There are different ways to lead in and out.

Words are often used to lead into the silence, usually a short passage from scripture or a religious book, or a poem. The words should encourage us to become open to some aspect of God as the focus for our contemplation, rather than to think about God (to meditate). One word, phrase or image may stand out for us, to hold as our focus. When our mind wanders (as it will), we just bring it back to that focus.

A mantra helps some people focus during contemplation. This is a word or phrase (for example, Jesus; Maranatha, come Lord Jesus; Lord have mercy; be still and know that I am God) repeated slowly in our head throughout the silence, in rhythm with our breathing, allowing it to go deep within us.

Breathing—just being aware of our breathing, in and out, helps many people to centre down into contemplation.

Music can lead in and out of contemplation, particularly where issues of language might make words inappropriate, as in bilingual or multi-ethnic groups. A gong or a 'singing bowl' may be used, again avoiding words which can be too specific.

A symbol may be used as a focus, either on its own or with words or music. As well as, or instead of, a candle, some people use a picture or icon as a visual focus. Many religious, created or natural objects can be a visual focus, or a tactile focus when held in the hand. Scent from herbs, flowers or incense may be used.

After the silence many Julian Meetings have tea and coffee and a time of sharing, while some maintain the silence as they leave.

Some Julian Meetings organise an annual Quiet Day, perhaps joining with other local Meetings. There are also occasional regional or national events.

There are over 300 Julian Meetings in Great Britain, and some worldwide. The JM Magazine and GB Newsletter are published in April, August and December, and anyone who is interested may subscribe for £6 per year. There are also booklets with helpful advice, both about contemplative prayer in general, and the Julian Meetings in particular, plus publicity material for Meetings to use.

Julian Meetings are ecumenical, open to people of all denominations or none, as long as they accept that the Meetings are Christ-centred. Most members are also part of a local Christian congregation. No method is taught: people are encouraged to explore what may be right for them.

Sharing prayerful silence with like-minded people can be both encouraging and strengthening. The whole group benefits when different people lead in and out of the silence, bringing their own insights and ideas. There can develop an intensity and depth to the shared silence that is not describable, but can only be experienced.

For more information either visit our website www.julianmeetings.org or send a stamped addressed envelope to The Julian Meetings, 263 Park Lodge Lane, Wakefield, West Yorkshire WF1 4HY.

BRF Quiet Days

BRF Quiet Days are an ideal way of redressing the balance in our busy lives. Held in peaceful locations around the country, each one is led by an experienced speaker and gives the opportunity to reflect, be silent and pray, and through it all to draw closer to God.

Wednesday 2 September: 'Contemplative Minister' led by Ian Cowley at Ripon College, Cuddesdon, Oxford, OX44 9EX

Wednesday 30 September: 'Being There' led by Debbie Thrower at Green Pastures, 17 Burton Road, Poole, Dorset, BH13 6DT

Saturday 17 October: 'Finding God in the Everyday' led by Naomi Starkey at The Trinity Centre, Church Road, Meole Brace, Shrewsbury, Shropshire, SY3 9HF

Monday 30 November: 'Behold, I am coming soon' led by Rodney Holder at the House of Retreat, The Street, Pleshey, Chelmsford, Essex, CM3 1HA

For further details and to book, please go to www.brfonline.org.uk/events-and-quiet-days or contact us at BRF, 15 The Chambers, Vineyard, Abingdon, Oxfordshire, OX14 3FE; tel: 01865 319700

Direct Debit

You can pay for your annual subscription to BRF notes using Direct Debit. You need to give your bank details only once, and the payment is made automatically every year until you cancel it. If you would like to pay by Direct Debit, please use the form opposite, entering your BRF account number under 'Reference'.

You are fully covered by the Direct Debit Guarantee:

The Direct Debit Guarantee

- This Guarantee is offered by all banks and building societies that accept instructions to pay Direct Debits.
- If there are any changes to the amount, date or frequency of your Direct Debit, The Bible Reading Fellowship will notify you 10 working days in advance of your account being debited or as otherwise agreed. If you request The Bible Reading Fellowship to collect a payment, confirmation of the amount and date will be given to you at the time of the request.
- If an error is made in the payment of your Direct Debit, by The Bible Reading Fellowship or your bank or building society, you are entitled to a full and immediate refund of the amount paid from your bank or building society.
  - If you receive a refund you are not entitled to, you must pay it back when The Bible Reading Fellowship asks you to.
- You can cancel a Direct Debit at any time by simply contacting your bank or building society. Written confirmation may be required. Please also notify us.

Quiet Spaces Subscription

Please note one-year subscription prices below include postage and packing.

You can also purchase your subcription by Direct Debit. Complete the details on the direct debit form and post to BRF with the order form.

Please send *Quiet Spaces* beginning with the January 2016/May 2016/ September 2016 issue (delete as applicable).

PRICES FOR UK ADDRESSES

DESCRIPTION	PRICE	QUANTITY ORDERED	TOTAL
Individual 1-year subscription includes postage and packing	£16.35		
Group 1-year subscription postage and packing FREE	£12.90		
ORDER TOTAL			

PRICES FOR OVERSEAS ADDRESSES—INCLUDES POSTAGE & PACKING

DESCRIPTION	PRICE	QUANTITY ORDERED	TOTAL
Individual 1-year subscription Standard	£27.60		
Individual 1-year subscription Europe and economy	£24.00		
ORDER TOTAL			

Prices are correct at time of going to press and subject to change.
For information about group subscriptions, see overleaf or contact BRF at the address given on the next page.

Promo code: QS0315

Method of payment

☐ Cheque ☐ MasterCard ☐ Maestro ☐ Visa ☐ Postal Order

Card no. ☐☐☐☐ ☐☐☐☐ ☐☐☐☐ ☐☐☐☐ ☐☐☐☐

Shaded boxes for Maestro use only

Valid from ☐☐☐☐ Expires ☐☐☐☐ Issue No. (Switch only) ☐☐☐☐

Security code* ☐☐☐ (Last 3 digits on the reverse of the card / *Essential in order to process your order*) 0000 **000** EXAMPLE

Signature .... Date ...... / ...... / ....

All subscription orders must be accompanied by the appropriate payment.
Please note: do not send payments for group orders. All group orders will be invoiced.

Name ....

Acc. No. ....

Address ....

.... Postcode ....

Telephone ....

Email ....

If you and a minimum of four friends subscribe to *Quiet Spaces* or BRF's other Bible reading notes (*New Daylight, Day by Day with God, Guidelines, The Upper Room*), you can form a group. What's so good about being in a group? You pay the price of the notes only—postage is free for delivery to a UK address. (All notes are sent to one address.) All group orders are invoiced. No advance payment is required. For more information, see www.biblereadingnotes.org.uk/group-subscriptions/ or contact the BRF office.

BRF, 15 The Chambers, Vineyard, Abingdon OX14 3FE;
Tel: 01865 319700   Fax: 01865 319701
www.brf.org.uk   email: enquiries@brf.org.uk
BRF is a Registered Charity (no: 233280)

The Bible Reading Fellowship

Instruction to your bank or building society to pay by Direct Debit

DIRECT Debit

Please fill in the whole form using a ballpoint pen and send to The Bible Reading Fellowship, 15 The Chambers, Vineyard, Abingdon OX14 3FE.

Service User Number: 5 5 8 2 2 9

Name and full postal address of your bank or building society

To: The Manager ....

.... Bank/Building Society

Address ....

....

.... Postcode ....

Name(s) of account holder(s)

Branch sort code

☐☐ – ☐☐ – ☐☐

Bank/Building Society account no.

☐☐☐☐☐☐☐☐

Reference

☐☐☐☐☐☐☐

Instruction to your Bank/Building Society

Please pay The Bible Reading Fellowship Direct Debits from the account detailed in this instruction, subject to the safeguards assured by the Direct Debit Guarantee. I understand that this instruction may remain with The Bible Reading Fellowship and, if so, details will be passed electronically to my bank/building society.

Signature(s)

Date

Banks and Building Societies may not accept Direct Debit instructions for some types of account.